Contract Theory
and the
Status of the Individual
in
Suarez (1548-1617)
and
Locke (1632-1704)

Jean-Paul Coujou

En Route Books and Media, LLC
Saint Louis, MO

En Route Books and Media, LLC
5705 Rhodes Avenue
St. Louis, MO 63109

Contact us at
contactus@enroutebooksandmedia.com

Cover Credit: Sebastian Mahfood

Copyright 2026 Jean-Paul Coujou

ISBN-13: 979-8-88870-551-3
Library of Congress Control Number:
Available online at https://catalog.loc.gov

All rights reserved. No part of this book may be reproduced, stored in a retrieval system, or transmitted in any form, or by any means, electronic, mechanical, photocopying, or otherwise, without the prior written permission of the author.

Table of Contents

Table of Contents

Preface

For both Suarez (1548-1617) and Locke (1632-1704), man's original condition is one of freedom, equality, and independence. Consequently, the difficulty facing all political questioning is how to understand the sources of the legitimacy of civil authority, given that by nature men are born free; how, then, to reconcile what is constitutive of the human mode of being with the necessity of political subjugation, and the position that no one is originally entitled to dominate his fellow man?

Introduction

Second Scholasticism, and Suarez's work in particular, through its critical examination of the fundamental concepts of politics (the natural condition of men, natural law, the law of nature, the social pact, the state, natural liberty and civil liberty ...) constitutes one of the most significant perspectives for accounting for the influence of Spanish Golden Age thought in seventeenth-century England, marked by "the awakening of Thomism," according to Quentin Skinner's evocative formula.[1] This filiation in the development of modern political philos-

---

[1] Q. SKINNER, *The Foundations of Modern Political Thought*, 2 vol., Cambridge, Cambridge University Press, 1978 (Les fondements de la pensée politique moderne, Paris, Albin Michel, 2001, traduction par J. Grossman & J.-Y. Pouilloux, II, 2ème partie, 5, p. 545). See also J.-F. Spitz, *John Locke et les fondements de la liberté moderne*, PUF, Paris, 2001, Ch. I, pp. 43–53 ; F. T., Baciero Ruiz, *Poder, ley y sociedad en Suárez y Locke.* (*Un capítulo en la evolución de la filosofía política del siglo XVII*), Ediciones Universidad de Salamanca, Salamanca, 2008, CD-ROM.

ophy could appear contradictory at first glance, if we were to limit ourselves to the condemnation in London in 1613 of Suarez's polemical *Defensio fidei christianas adversus anglicanae sectae errores*[2] (because it represented a threat to royal power), which was directed against James I's political and religious ambitions.

Beyond these historical considerations, a continuity and a point of convergence concerning the criticism of royal absolutism can immediately be identified in the political philosophies of Suarez and Locke, based on Filmer's (1588-1653) critique of Suarez's positions and Locke's criticism of Filmer. On the one hand, in the first book of his *Patriarca or the naturel power of Kings* (published posthumously in 1680),[3] Filmer wrote a refutation of Car-

---

[2] SUAREZ, *Defensio Fidei. De anglicana secta*, *Opera Omnia* (O. O.), éditions Vivès, Paris, 1856–1877, 28 volumes, volume 24, Books III et VI.

[3] R. FILMER, *Patriarca*, Paris, L'Harmattan, 2004, dir. P. Thierry. As said by A. Díaz Vera, Los liberales *radicales ingleses y la filosofía política de Francisco Suárez in Proceso de mercado*: *Revista europea de Economía Política*, Vol. XVI, n° 1, Primavera 2019, p. 158, Filmer men-

dinal Bellarmine's theses on the question of the supremacy of the Pope over the King,[4] while in the second book, because it was deemed "unnatural," he opposed the Suarezian thesis that the people choose or elect their rulers and, consequently, the possibility of a mixed or limited monarchy.[5] For Filmer, this means rejecting the contractualist theses of both authors concerning the origin of political power, implying the possibility of a legitimate popular revolt against civil power in the case of proven tyranny. The theological-political consequences would be: the pernicious questioning of civil authority and

---

mentions Suarez 13 times and Bellarmine 20 times in his book. See also: J. DUNN, *The Political Thought of John Locke*, Cambridge, Cambridge University Press, 1969, Part 2, Ch. VI, (J. Dunn, *La pensée politique de John Locke*, PUF, Léviathan, Paris, 1991, traduction par J.-F. Baillon, 2ème partie, Ch. VI, p. 67–84.)

[4] R. BELLARMINE, *On temporal and spiritual authority*, Liberty Fund, Indianapolis, 2012, edited and with an introduction by Stefania Tutino, *On Laymen or Secular People*, Ch. 10 to 13, *On the Temporal power of the Pope. Against William Barclay*, and *On the primary duty of the supreme Pontiff*, p. 409–419.

[5] SUAREZ, *De Legibus* (O. O.), volume 5, Book III.

the excessive promotion of papal authority. On the other hand, Locke, in his *Treatise on Civil Government* (1680),[6] criticizes Filmer's critique, taking as his starting point the refutation of the thesis of the divine justification of the king's absolute power; this thesis invokes the refusal of political consent between the rulers and the ruled, based on the analogy between the monarch and the father of the family, each exercising full authority over either his subjects or his children. For Locke, the erroneous nature of Filmer's theses and their theoretical weakness can be reduced to two statements: that a political government can never be anything other than an absolute monarchy, and that man possesses no natural freedom.[7] Once we have recognized that civil authority must not be confused with paternal authority (even if the divine act of creation determines it),

---

[6] J. LOCKE, *Two treatises of government*, Everyman's Library. Introduction by Professor W.S. Carpenter, 1982. (*Deuxième traité du gouvernement civil*, Paris, Vrin, 1977, traduction par B. Gilson). Et *Traité du gouvernement civil*, Paris, Garnier-Flammarion, 1992, traduction de D. Mazel, introduction par S. Goyard-Fabre.)

[7] *Ibid.*, Ier traité, Ch. 1, p. 46.

we need to explain the origin, scope, and purpose of civil government according to Locke.

Leaving aside Suarez's and Locke's refutation of royal absolutism, what appears decisive in making the workings of political society intelligible according to the constitution of their respective theories of the nature and origin of power in its articulation with human nature, concerns the problem of consent to the law. To what extent can and should politics as a public relationship between men be understood in terms of domination and the obligation to obey? At the source of this recomposition of political questioning - and it is in this sense that Skinner aptly invokes "a revival of Thomism" - is the question formulated by Thomas Aquinas concerning, in the state of innocence, a possible domination of men over one another.[8] The term domination has two meanings. Either a situation of subjection of the slave to the master, the former being merely a means to the latter's utility and satisfaction, or the

[8] THOMAS D'AQUIN, *Somme théologique*, édition coordonnée par A. Raulin, traduction par A. M. Roguet, 4 volumes, Paris, Cerf, 1984–1986, Iª, Q. 96, art. 4.

exercise of superiority by the one whose aim is to govern and guide free men. In this case, man becomes his own end, and political existence acquires its raison d'être when the domination exercised over a free man has no other purpose than to direct the latter towards the common good. In the absence of the latter, human multiplicity could not become one. This is why - and why there can be no reconciliation between law, freedom, and power - as Saint Augustine reminds us, quoted by Thomas Aquinas: "the just command not because they aspire to dominate, but because they wish to serve by their wisdom; this is what the order of nature prescribes, and this is how God created man."[9]

Consequently, the power of constraint conveyed by the notion of domination is what makes the political bond effective, since in its absence, no government of men would be conceivable, since respect

---

[9] AUGUSTIN, SAINT, *La cité de Dieu*, Editions du Seuil, Paris, 1994, traduction de L. Moreau revue par J.-C. Eslin, 3 volumes, volume 3, livre XIX, XIV, p. 125 :" Car ce n'est point par la passion de dominer qu'ils commandent, mais par la loi du dévouement, non par orgueil d'être le maître, mais par le devoir de la providence. »

for the boundary between what must be done and what must be abstained from cannot be guaranteed. Politics, which concerns community life and relations between communities and between communities and individuals, refers to the constitution of political bodies endowed with specific powers, a will to order the multiple and rules of existence corresponding to laws.[10] Nevertheless, for both Suárez and Locke, force and the power of constraint are legitimate in politics only if they are at the service of law. The coercion of law cannot claim a legitimacy external to the preservation of law, whose existence and raison d'être it does not underpin, since the value of the rules of justice pre-exists their conventional establishment. It is possible for politics not to be reducible to a de facto state of confrontation between powers, and in which what appears to be primary is of the order of value, as demonstrated by the theses on natural law and natural right. Thus,

---

[10] SUÁREZ, *De Legibus*, (*O. O.*) volume 5, Book III, 2, n. 4, p. 181:" For it is impossible to conceive of a united body politic without political government and organization. »

the establishment and enforcement of laws is a means at the service of a human community whose value can be understood in light of a rational norm of law pre-existing civil laws. As man is by nature a political animal, there is a necessity for civil existence before its historical incarnations in various forms of government. Civil laws consist in giving effect to the higher law that every man, being a man and endowed with reason, always already knows in conscience; they have authority only because they are compatible with the law of nature, which is intrinsically just and reasonable, and the sign of a divine will that exceeds the human will.

In this sense, ethics and politics, while two distinct domains, are indissociable. Reason lacks sufficient guiding force to unite mankind, reflecting the weakness and inadequacy of moral obligation. It can, however, assume one, based on the natural yet reasonable need to structure the human world into a political one, in accordance with the principles of human nature. However, a political community can as easily make reasonable or unreasonable use of force by providing itself with the means to ensure respect; this is why such use receives its ethical measure from its adequacy to the law of nature. Thus, in demonstrating their freedom and capacity for reason, human beings nonetheless reveal that their mode of being is not necessarily reasonable. For Suarez and Locke, understanding the political requires a differentiation between the constitutive fact of men's condition as only able to be publicly together, and the historical and positive form that a government will take. On the one hand, political association is referred to, at its foundation, as a natural community, a universal reality inherent in human nature that imposes itself by necessity, regardless of the institutional conditions that diversify its historical manifestations. On the other hand, without the coercive power of laws, such an association would have no guarantee of its effective duration or of its demand for peace and justice.

The law of nature in this process of differentiation cannot be a sufficient condition for rendering a system of positive law effective, which is tantamount to recognizing that political society can necessarily be likened to a human construct, with power having no source other than the collectivity of men.[11] To this end, human ability to legislate and establish lasting communities must be related to the referent of what immediately exists and is given, like things, namely the natural condition of men and the state of nature, which is its infra-political space of externalization.[12] We must therefore explain the theoretical link, and its practical consequences, between the legitimacy of the law of nature and the conventional nature of positive law. For both Suarez and Locke, man's original condition is one of freedom, equality, and independence. Consequently, the difficulty facing all political questioning is how to understand the sources of the legitimacy of civil authority,[13] given that by nature men are born free;[14] how, then, to reconcile what is constitutive of

---

[11] *Ibid.*, n. 4, p. 181.

[12] *Ibid.*, 1, n. 2, p. 176:" The civil magistracy with temporal power to govern men is just and perfectly in keeping with human nature.»

[13] *Ibid.*, 1, n. 1, p. 176:" The problem is this: can men, if we stick exclusively to the nature of things, give orders to other men and oblige them by means of their own laws?»

[14] *Ibid.*, n. 1, p. 176.

the human mode of being with the necessity of political subjugation, and the position that no one is originally entitled to dominate his fellow man?[15]

---

[15] *Ibid.* Et SAINT AUGUSTIN, *La Cité de Dieu*, volume 3, livre XIX, XV, p. 126 :" Car la plus cruelle domination qui ravage le cœur des mortels, n'est-ce pas entre autres la passion de dominer ? ».

I

Human Nature and the Power of Reason

According to Suarez and Locke, it is up to every political society, from its natural origin and its artificial construction, to implement the means likely to manage and orient a state of affairs stemming from human nature, without these same means coinciding with the primary and immediate way of being of men, or with what the unhindered development of their nature could have produced. As Suarez synthesizes[1] from Saint Augustine,[2] political power is not consubstantial with the natural given; it does not mean that it is contrary to nature.[3] Political society is the result of human conventions. Still, they are ordered by a natural principle, teleologically

---

[1] *Ibid.*, III, 1, n. 12, p. 179.

[2] SAINT AUGUSTIN, *La cité de Dieu*, volume 3, livre XIX, XV, p. 125–127.

[3] SUÁREZ, *De Legibus*, (*O. O.*) volume 5, Book III, 1, n. 12, p. 179

oriented towards the perfection of the human mode of being, through its ordering towards the common good. But the specificity of the latter is such that it pre-exists as a value in the laws designed to actualize it, while at the same time delimiting and grounding the legitimacy of institutional means; in its original absence, the human community would diffract into an erratic and aimless multiplicity.

Consequently, in the Suarezian perspective, a chiasmus must be operated: it is not the convention that determines the possibility and value of the common good, but the common good that imposes itself as the principle of the legitimacy of any convention. Pre-existent to its legislative incarnation, it is constitutive of the definition of man as a political animal, and inherent to the goal assigned to all human groupings, namely, the fulfillment of the human in man. By the same token, an analogy can be drawn between the metaphysical and political orders. According to the first order, essence is the specific determination according to which the fact of existing in act becomes possible; it constitutes the very reason for being, and corresponds for Suarez to the real essence that has by itself the possibility of existing in act. In the sphere of created being, reality is grasped as the movement of the possible towards its realization. Thus, essence posits reality as capable of being distinguished from the effectivity of the created thing, and the possibility of thinking the created thing is inseparable from effectivity. Existence in act, however, is not really part of the possible, but is inherent in the effectivity of every being. Essence is a possible being capable of effective existence, and therefore inseparable from real being. Consequently, the essence of a finite being is identifiable with a real essence. In the political order, the common good is to social existence what essence is to existence. To exist for the common good is to be its essence in act, through the mediation of the political institution. Politics must be the moment when essence in act is equivalent to existence, i.e., when the existence of the common good adds nothing to its essence in act. The state must consecrate the moment when, for the common good, essence and existence are identified in reality.

The instrument of this mediation can only be the law, made effective by political power. Indeed, political power exists only insofar as it has the authority to establish laws that guide and direct how citizens live. Even if man is naturally sociable, individuals are not originally capable of spontaneous, let alone lasting, agreement, which confirms not only that political power is consistent with human nature, but also that it necessarily results from it,[4] without men being able to form a body politic from the outset. For Suarez,[5] the theological view that the source of power is original sin must be replaced by the anthropological thesis that the natural human way of life, which involves being with others, cannot be perfected without the power of a binding bond that enables each individual to direct his or her own conduct without prejudice. In accordance with the Platonic thesis, political existence exceeds social existence because it does not reduce its essential raison d'être to the material satisfaction of needs, but is the quest for a better life understood as a hap-

---

[4] *Ibid.*, n. 2, p. 176.

[5] SUÁREZ, *De opere sex dierum* (O. O.), volume 3, Book V, 7, n. 6, pp. 414–415. Per una traduzione in italiano del libro V, vedi C. FARACO, *Trattato dell'Opera dei Sei Giorni. Libro Quinto*, Capua, Arteteta edizione, 2015, pp. 36–43.

py life together, indissociable from communication and exchange in line with rectitude, inherent in what human nature tends towards.[6] To grasp its scope, we need to produce a genealogy of political society, based on an analysis of the specificity of the different levels of human community to which the definition of man as a social animal refers, while drawing on the Aristotelian heritage and differentiating between the state of innocence and the state of pure nature.[7] To posit that man naturally tends to live in community requires recognizing a dual human community: one imperfect or familial and the other perfect or political, i.e., fully autonomous. The first is totally natural and original, by the very fact that it is the material condition of all begetting and continuity of life: it corresponds to the union of man and woman, without which the preservation of the human race would be inconceivable. It comprises three moments. 1°) The first is a community of life, implying spontaneity, a first and indisputable

---

[6] *Ibid.*, p. 415.

[7] SUÁREZ, *De Legibus* (O. O.), volume 5, Book III, 1, n. 3, pp. 176–177.

manifestation of life. It is the first way in which human beings appear to one another, confirming for Suárez that man cannot achieve his own humanity in solitude, which only makes sense through the recognition of the omnipresence of others. And the other is the neighbor, a self that appears as an extension, an analog of myself, asserting itself against the backdrop of an original link to others. 2°) In the second stage, with the family, this bond is reinforced by the function of parental education, without which existence could not be self-sufficient; this is the moment when the conditions for future autonomy are created through the repeated use of theoretical and practical reason. 3°) The association of families gave rise to the first forms of society involving relations of dependence or subjection. Because man is an *ens in alio* and can only be what he is characterized by humanity understood as nature, every individual is reducible to the fulfillment of a genus, originally linked to other individuals of an identical genus. And extending this to the human mode of being and ethics, we can say that, to belong to the human race, men require the help, mediation, and guidance of other men.[8]

These three moments in the development of the imperfect community involve a form of union that finds its fulfillment in the political community. Imperfection, specific to the first of these communities, is surpassed in the perfection of the city-state as an autonomous union. What is given at the beginning contains within it the end that gives it its raison d'être, the affirmation of the human being as the principle of his own development, or as *ens per se*. If the family represents a provisionally autonomous moment of private and domestic existence, it cannot, because of the ontological status of the individual and in view of the development of the human race, be self-sufficient. This is precisely what the universal reality of human work and exchange confirms. No family can produce sufficient means to meet the indispensable needs for the perfection of human life.[9] and the growth of the forces and knowledge required for it.

---

[8] *Ibid.*, p. 177.

[9] *Ibid.*

Added to this is the fact that the division of humankind into scattered families constitutes an obstacle to lasting peace between men, as there are no means of limiting and punishing injustice,[10] and consequently of subjecting those who transgress the rules to the imperatives of the common good through recourse to public power. This is why, as Suarez reminds us, the ancients, such as Cicero,[11] asserted that by establishing an ordered and autonomous community, bound by law, mankind comes as close as possible to the divine order. Through politics, human beings help to actualize the universal nature of reason, despite their finitude. In this way, the human community is realized in a state resulting from the association of different cities, embodying in this movement, in the same way as reason, that which is most adequate to the realization of the human race. Indeed, the state is an autonomous community that requires a governing

---

[10] *Ibid.*

[11] *Ibid.* Et Cicéron, *De la république*, Paris, Garnier-Flammarion, 1965, traduction par Ch. Appuhn, livre VI, ch. 13, p. 111.

power, without which the human bond can only become corrupted. An analogy makes this clear: just as nature provides what is necessary for man, the autonomous community, by virtue of its conformity to reason and, consequently, to the principles of natural law, makes it possible, thanks to the type of power it engenders, to produce what is necessary for the human bond to escape generalized disorder.[12] But, of course, human beings do not create a single political community; they only constitute an aggregate of multiple domestic unions[13] by accident, which cannot claim the title of moral unity. For the latter to be effective as a lasting inter-human bond, a multiplicity must voluntarily set itself the goal of the common good,[14] a conjunction of order, virtue, and a happy life. The common good can be identi-

---

[12] *Ibid.* And CICERON, *De la république*, Paris, Garnier-Flammarion, 1965, traduction par Ch. Appuhn, livre VI, ch. 13, p. 111.

[13] SUAREZ, *De opere sex dierum* (O. O.), volume 3, Book V, 7, n. 3, p. 414.

[14] SUAREZ, *Defensio Fidei,* (O. O.), Volume 24, III, 2, n. 6, p. 208.

fied with an end that is not naturally realized, but towards which it is up to man to strive.

This cannot conceal the following paradox: it does not depend on men, in view of their creaturely nature and the multiplication of exchanges, not to give themselves political power. Nevertheless, it does depend on them, in conforming to the commandment of natural reason, to configure it in such a way that it participates in the common good, to turn a primary necessity into a fully assumed freedom. Freedom understood politically does not reside in a fictitious autonomy regarding the laws of human nature, but rather in the exact determination of the creature's essence, and in the possibility offered on this basis of actualizing it for appropriate ends. To say that man is a social animal. A political one means that he is not free to be so, but that the intellection of such a necessity is already the condition for a causality by freedom to express itself. Politics implies that man externalizes the freedom of his will with full knowledge of the facts. It cannot, therefore, be dissociated from man's mastery over himself, based on knowledge of the necessities of his nature, i.e., on the power to choose from what he did not originally choose: to be a political animal. This is also why political existence must be seen as the result of historical development. Ultimately, man shows himself to be all the more specific the more he brings out what separates him from his original condition, from nature and animality. Political existence confirms that human nature is not properly natural, since it is not realized naturally, i.e., immediately, spontaneously, and necessarily, nor can it impose itself as an external order; indeed, such a nature cannot become effective without the production of conventions and recourse to practice. Such an existence integrates its own end within itself: security, freedom, peace, justice, and prosperity.

Man's uprooting from his original condition - the ability with which he is originally endowed - presents political existence precisely as man-made; paradoxically, man is a creator insofar as he does not wish to be original, i.e., the source of what enables him to be what he is. For Suarez, the explanatory and operative concept presiding over the understanding of human nature is the state of nature (or the natural condition of men,[15] which disregards grace), according to which the foundation of the ethical and political bond between men will be examined. The state of nature expresses not so much a pre-political state as the reality inherent to all social creation: the imperfection and finiteness of the individual, who requires others to fulfill his humanity. Its function is to free man's original situation from its theological reduction, to determine human nature in terms of its three fundamental components: freedom, reason, and finitude.[16] This means bracketing references to sin or disorder, and taking man's natural condition as the sole point of reference.[17] The latter, as we have already explained, corresponds to the fact that man is a social animal, and requires, by his very nature as a human being, "a communal way of life that a public power must necessarily govern."[18] Nevertheless, from a theological

---

[15] SUAREZ, *De Legibus* (O. O.), volume 5, Book III, 1, n. 12, p. 179. And *De gratia, O. O.*, volume 7, Prolegomenum IV, *De statibus humanae naturae*, 1, n. 5, p. 180.

[16] *Ibid.*, Book II, 8, n. 4, p. 117.

[17] *Ibid.*, Book III, 1, n. 12, p. 179.

[18] *Ibid.*

point of view, man's first state corresponds to a state of innocence comparable to a situation of axiological neutrality, during which human freedom remains subordinate to the infinite power of the Creator.[19]

This state of innocence is based on a representation of the human being founded on the separation between the finite and the infinite. Such a separation expresses: 1°) the seal of the infinite being on the finite being, and 2°) the fact that man's natural condition implies his confrontation with the universality and necessity of his political and historical dimension. If we consider the second point of separation, he reminds us that humankind possesses the ability to appeal to the command of natural reason, or critical intelligence, to guarantee both its preservation and its self-determination.[20] However, the purpose of these commands can only be realized if mankind unites politically and establishes an au-

---

[19] SUÁREZ, *De opere sex dierum* (O. O.), volume 3, Book III, pp. 170–324.

[20] SUÁREZ, *De Legibus* (O. O.), volume 5, Book III, 3, n. 5, p. 183.

tonomous community.[21] The natural condition carries with it its own transcendence, and the political cannot be considered an accidental property of man. What makes it possible for man to detach himself from his natural condition is not man's doing, for man is not the foundation of man, since he was created in the image and likeness of God. Thus, the natural condition that gives rise to man's humanity does not refer to a nature that man gives to himself; it exceeds and precedes him. This condition is secondary to man's immediate nature, yet primary to the particularity of his nature. The theme of the natural condition clarifies the particular nature of the individual when he reaches his universal humanity, or a properly human mode of being. This nature is transcendent, because it constitutes the origin and foundation of every individual, by virtue of its radical exteriority; it is immanent, because it is inherent in the very fact of being human. The natural condition means that it is universal for human beings to detach themselves from natural immediacy, which precisely enables them to particularize

---

[21] *Ibid.*, n. 6, p. 183.

themselves through the variable forms they can give to their coexistence. From then on, it's up to man's natural condition to confirm that nothing is naturally human, that the advent of humanity is historical and political. Therefore, living together, in accordance with the Aristotelian heritage, is natural. And because man is a political animal, the existence of the state cannot constitute an obstacle or a limitation; it simply confirms that man does not have the power to be totally what he is, since the realization of what he must be is conditional on the mediation of being-in-common. As a result, the state is not the effect of a consensus, but rather a transformation of this natural condition in the course of history.

In the light of these considerations, Suarez and Locke share a common requirement for the renewal of political theory: a history of civil power that takes the origin of political power as its starting point. On the one hand, for Suarez, the emergence of political power can only be envisaged from the moment when multiple families began to associate to form an autonomous community.[22] It is clear from the

[22] *Ibid.*, 2, n. 3, p. 180.

theological account that such a community could not have come into existence either with the creation of Adam, or by the will of those who became part of it, and that Adam himself could not claim any political supremacy in such a community; this cannot be deduced from any natural principle. In this history of political power, theology is not a relevant recourse for producing an intelligibility that accounts for the real history of human relations. A fallacious interpretation of the person of Adam leads us to forget the primary truth that the Creator did not directly or indirectly grant any man sovereign power or the power to govern his fellow men politically.[23]

So, if power exists only in and through men, it does not exist in any individual particularity, but only in the collectivity.[24] The consequence of this is to split the representation of the human community. 1°) At the outset, mankind is a pure aggregate of individualities (with no physical or moral structure) not subject to a common power, yet with the ability

---

[23] *Ibid.*

[24] *Ibid.*, n. 4, p. 181.

to bring one into being; the ordering of this community is only potential, without being able to actually exist historically. This first moment implies that sovereign power does not exist, strictly speaking, but only in potential.[25] 2°) Men institute an autonomous political body, presupposing order and authority, "by a specific act of its will or a common consent" identifiable with a "unique mystical body"[26] (a unity per se, ethical and political, organized with a view to the common good) historically actualizing a sovereign power vis-à-vis which, henceforth, it no longer depends on individuals when they are socially stakeholders, not to accept it. Legislative power, the link par excellence, is precisely what makes the shift from nature to history intelligible, since it does not by nature belong to the community or to any particular individual at the outset, without which there would be a negation of the principle of equality and freedom between men.[27] The law is the only way to move from a natu-

---

[25] *Ibid.*

[26] *Ibid.*

[27] *Ibid.*, 3, n. 1, p. 182.

ral, de facto multiplicity to a political, historically instituted unity of law. The original democracy to which Suárez refers, therefore, expresses the fact that men (or the people), in expressing their resolve to unite in a political body, determine from this founding principle the basic structure from which all other political forms will be sketched out. It means that it is up to the people, through their constituent power, to assume the founding responsibility for the institution in deed of political power, and that they thereby possess the legitimacy to ensure that the exercise of this power does not exceed the limits of the function entrusted to them, namely the common good. Original democracy presupposes that humankind possesses a specific social unity, which it will historically actualize through the institution of a legislative power. The latter can only be the attribute of the community as a whole, which in turn establishes political power over all individuals. The original power of the people over itself can only be achieved historically by turning into a sovereign external power over the people, which is to say that while it originally belongs to the people to depend on itself, such an origin does not coincide with the conditions of possibility of the exercise of power, implying that it does not depend on the people to depend directly on itself. In answering the question of the origin of power, another question inevitably arises: who, legitimately, should exercise it without freedom and equality being trampled underfoot?

On the other hand, for Locke, as for Suarez, it is necessary to reject 1°) the thesis of paternity and property as sources of sovereignty[28] and 2°) the conception of monarchy as an inheritance transmitted by Adam.[29] This is the prerequisite for uncovering the true genesis of government and providing the means to determine who is in a position to exercise power legitimately. In fact, paternal power is limited in time and has no other function than to train children in reason and freedom; it is a duty to educate humanity, reminding us that "*Understanding* that sets Man above the rest of sensible Beings."[30] In the

---

[28] J. LOCKE, *Two treatises of government*, Book I, Ch. VII, § 73–77, p. 51-56.

[29] *Ibid.*, Ch. IX, § 81–103, p. 58–71.

[30] J. LOCKE, *An essay concerning human understanding*, Clarendon Press-Oxford, edited with a foreword by P.-H. Niddich, 1975, Introduction, p. 44.

private sphere, this power concerns beings who are not yet reasonable; nevertheless, the ends it pursues cannot be juxtaposed with the public ends of politics, which must presuppose, to be justified, free, equal, and reasonable beings. Finally, we need to differentiate between the transmission of power and that of property. Political power aims to establish a general good that is not subject to any transmission, and property a particular good that can therefore be transferred without prejudice. As for the figure of Adam, because the Creator is said to have given him power over all creatures, it in no way constitutes a reference point to justify a despotic power, that of an absolute monarch who would be his heir. This contradicts the political nature of power by presenting earthly government as a combination of force and violence,[31] and consequently leads human relations into an endless logic of reversibility between

---

[31] J. LOCKE, *Essais sur la loi de nature*, Bibliothèque de philosophie Politique de l'Université de Caen, Caen, 1986, Essai I, p. 17 :" (…) Les magistrats pourraient, sans doute, contraindre la multitude à l'obéissance par la violence et par les armes, mais ils ne pourraient pas l'obliger. »

dominator and dominated, servitude and liberation, order suffered and revolt aimed at overthrowing it.

Once these confusions have been cleared up, to gain a proper understanding of political power and clarify the path by which it has historically imposed itself, it is necessary to return to the natural condition of men[32] - identifiable with the state of nature - which, without being asocial or presocial, is nonetheless ahistorical, even if we cannot but recognize that history is the universal reality in which men are forced to live. This condition refers to a state of affairs revealed by sensible experience, i.e., not to a hypothetical human nature, but rather to its empirical donation, which must be deciphered. In this sense, the state of nature can be defined neither by a state of war nor a political condition, for it is that

---

[32] J. LOCKE, *Two treatises of government*, Book II, Ch. II, n. 4, p. 118:" To understand political power aright, and derive it from its original, we must consider what estate all men are naturally in, and that is, a state of perfect freedom to order their actions, ad dispose of their possessions and persons as they think fit, within the bounds of the law of Nature, without asking leave or depending upon the will of any other man. »

moment when men coexist in accordance with reason and ignore any higher authority to settle their controversies.[33] Conversely, the state of war is the moment when relations between men are modified by force or subject to the permanent threat of force. It is also an apolitical situation, since the links between men are not ordered according to reciprocal conventions, the only ones capable of instituting a political society. For Locke, invoking a state of nature is tantamount to referring to a universal framework from which the raison d'être of law can emerge. But this is only relevant for Locke if we take into account the theological and anthropological implications of the Fall. On the one hand, original sin inscribes humanity in finitude; on the other, work is the consequence of this finitude, through the need it implies to respond practically to the renewal of life and to scarcity, while conferring a value on the things we enjoy in this world;[34] from this

---

[33] *Ibid.*, n. 19, p. 126.

[34] *Ibid.*, n. 42, p. 137.

derives property,[35] since through his work, man associates a part of himself with a given of nature and appropriates it.[36] According to the law of nature enacted by the Creator and binding on the whole human race, every individual retains ownership of his or her own person,[37] which means that no one may harm another's life, liberty, or possessions. And if God, in accordance with the position of the Salamanca School with Vitoria and Suarez, has made the world a common space for men,[38] He has also made them capable of reason, so that they may make the best use of it, given the limits of their condition and their spatial and temporal situation. Thus, the law of nature, by creating the basis for a shift from appropriation by labor to ownership, confronts man with the limits of the extension of

---

[35] *Ibid.*, n. 31, p. 131:" As much as anyone can make use of to any advantage of life before it spoils, so much he may by his labor fix a property in. Whatever is beyond this is more than his share and belongs to others. »

[36] *Ibid.*, n. 27, p. 130.

[37] *Ibid.*

[38] *Ibid.*, n. 26, p. 129.

the latter by "the voice of reason."[39] And while "the measure of property Nature will set, by the extent of men's labor and the conveniency of life,"[40] the effect of this division has been to generate insecurity and uncertainty about what had been acquired through labor, and the risk of recourse to force inherent in relations of dependence between men. It is therefore up to the law, in political society, to prevent all future evil,[41] because property lays the foundations for economic progress, but also for differentiation through wealth, which is a source of increased conflict between men, greed, corruption, envy, and the weakening of social morality. This is explained by "the desire of having more than men needed had altered the intrinsic value of things,"[42] which originated with the universal use of gold and silver; from then on, everyone had the legitimate possibility, without harming others, of appropriating more than they really needed. In this way, in the absence of any

---

[39] *Ibid.*, n. 31, p. 131.

[40] *Ibid.*, n. 36, p. 133.

[41] *Ibid.*, n. 20, p. 127.

[42] *Ibid.*, n. 37, p. 134.

contract and outside the original social bonds, humanity created a sharing of what was common and its transformation into a "disproportionate and unequal possession of the earth."[43]

Alongside these determinations, the state of nature also receives new light if we refer, as in Suarez, to the metaphysical concepts of real essence and existence and beings of reason, which, in Locke, amounts to articulating it with the question of real essence and the properties that derive from it. Indeed, the latter, as logical relations, express relations of physical causality or explanatory function of what is, by reference to origin. When analyzing the notion of a state of nature irreducible to the position of a historical origin, a distinction must be made between nominal and real essence, since, for Locke, only the former is capable of being known, the latter exceeding the capacities of the understanding.[44]

The causes of our limited knowledge lie either in a lack of ideas, or in a failure to apprehend the suit-

---

[43] *Ibid.*, n. 50, p. 140.

[44] J. LOCKE, *An Essay Concerning Human Understanding*, Book III, Ch. 6.

ability or unsuitability of ideas, or in a lack of method accompanied by excessive haste. Acknowledging these limitations inevitably raises questions about the function of language[45] in producing the notion of a state of nature, whose meaning is not focused on an unknowable historical situation, at the risk of falling back on the imperfections and abuses of language that result from forgetting that words refer to ideas, not things - in other words, of submitting to an erroneous theory of meaning. The point is to avoid misusing the term by not associating any precise idea with it, and to master its use by making it a means of intuitively determining the justification of political society, its imperatives, and the variation of its manifestations based on human conventions. To understand each other, we must assume that these terms "state of nature" designate an invariant real

[45] *Ibid.*, Book II, Ch. XXXIII, § 19, p. 401:" (...) I find, that there is so close a connexion between *Ideas* and Words; and our abstract *Ideas*, and general Words, have so constant a relation one to another, that is impossible to speak clearly and distinctly of our Knowledge, which all consists in Propositions, without considering, first, the Nature, Use, and Signification of Language. »

essence. We must then refer to a minimal meaning. To reach an agreement, such a term must be considered a supposition, not an idea that corresponds adequately to the facts. There will therefore be an error on the question, not from the moment we assume that this term designates a reality that can be attested, but by assuming that it does so through its real essence. And the expression "state of nature" will only be relevant in terms of the conformity of the term and the idea with the real existence of what is (civil government), without any claim to knowledge of its real essence in the absence of experience of such a state.

How, then, is the expression "state of nature" to be conceived, so that it does not constitute a parasitic element or a verbal illusion and, consequently, is not misused? If knowledge can be assimilated to the perception of relationships between ideas, it appears to be reduced to the sphere of ideas. We cannot, therefore, go beyond the ideas given by experience, whether we consider the experience of sensation or that of reflection. What then is the meaning of a state of nature that is not the object of possible experience? If we know only through the mediation of ideas, what is the criterion for distinguishing between "the extravagant imaginations that form in men's brains,"[46] the chimeras they forge in their minds, and ideas that actually correspond to reality? To do this, we need to distinguish between simple ideas, which are not fictions, but rather "natural and regular productions of Things without us, really operating upon us,"[47] and complex ideas, abstracting from those of substances and archetypes that the intellect has forged of its own accord. If we consider the ideas of substances, they are complex and relate to models external to us; this is why our knowledge of these ideas may not correspond to reality. The ideas of substances as combinations of simple ideas resulting from a deduction from the natural given, are able to differ from archetypes for the reason "by having more or different ideas united in them than are to be found united in the things themselves."[48]

---

[46] *Ibid.*, Book IV, Ch. 4, § 1, p. 562: "Is there any thing so extravagant, as the Imaginations of Men's Brains?"

[47] *Ibid.*, § 4, p. 564.

[48] *Ibid.*, § 11, p. 568.

The idea of a state of nature is complex and inevitably raises the question of its agreement with reality. To determine its specific status, we need to distinguish between general knowledge and singular knowledge, i.e., between knowledge formulated verbally by means of universal propositions and knowledge formulated verbally by means of singular propositions whose specific objects are God, the self, and the other. The universal propositions of which it is possible to produce certain knowledge are not linked to existence; the thesis of concordance or discordance between ideas applies to them without their being existential propositions, as is the case with mathematics. Regarding singular propositions, we have knowledge of ourselves through intuition, of the existence of God through demonstration, and of what is external to us through sensation. The idea of the state of nature is part of Locke's division between two kinds of knowledge. 1°) Universal, abstract and hypothetical knowledge of the relations between ideas, as in mathematics, morality and theology. 2°) Knowledge relating to particular existences, for which it is problematic to apply the principle of concordance or discordance between ideas. Nevertheless, the idea of the state of nature has a specific function in the order of universal propositions, in the sense that it has a practical, ethical and political scope. It serves as the original standard for assessing what should be done in a political society. As a model without donation in experience (this origin can be considered in the sense of that which made us, which has irretrievably separated and which we do not have the means to reach) it is this referent without which we could not evaluate the order of the fact. In the absence of such an archetype, man could not universally measure the progress he still has to make; what is empirically unobservable, is practically justified as a regulating model of ought-to-be.

In Suarez and Locke, this is precisely what is confirmed by the ordering of the state of nature to man's own law of nature, inscribed in the teleological and legal structure of the world created by God. Every creature acts according to a law that is in keeping with its nature. The law of nature rejects the very idea of a state of nature as a lawless situation; because its purpose is peace and the safeguarding of humankind through the pursuit of respect for equality and freedom, it guarantees the legitimacy of civil society, while confirming the theological basis of politics.[49]

[49] For LOCKE, see J. DUNN, *The Political Thought of John Locke,* Cambridge, Cambridge University Press, 1969; J. TULLY, *A discourse on Property: John Locke and his Adversaries*, Cambridge, Cambridge University Press, 1978. For SUAREZ, see J.-P. COUJOU, *Droit, anthropologie et politique chez Suárez*, Perpignan, Artège, 2012.

II

The Law of Nature and the Political Community

For both Suarez and Locke, the law of nature implies the Creator's seal on his creature, justifying, in this sense, Skinner's formula for the "revival of Thomism." According to the Thomist heritage, this concept expresses in human nature the call of the divine, reminding us that all that is subordinate to divine providence is also subordinate to the rule and measure of eternal law.[1] Human action is oriented towards the Creator, with each creature participating in the eternal law according to its mode of being,[2] i.e., it tends towards its specific act and end (which corresponds to persevering in its being) through the mediation of such a law. For a reasona-

[1] THOMAS D'AQUIN, *Somme théologique*, Ia–IIae, Q. 91, art. 2.

[2] *Ibid.*, Réponse: « Il est donc évident que la loi naturelle n'est pas autre chose qu'une participation de la loi éternelle dans la créature raisonnable. »

ble being,[3] the law is irreducible to a pure rule, since it originally manifests an obligation that is inseparable from its legitimacy, because it is founded on the imperatives of reason. Thus, the morality of human practice has a dual origin. Indeed, for Thomas Aquinas, about voluntary acts commanded by practical reason, it is appropriate to refer both to the inner principles directing moral practice and to the outer principles prescribing or forbidding man an action, i.e., the law, "an ordinance of reason with a view to the common good, promulgated by him who is in charge of the community."[4] Now, if law constitutes a rule of action as well as the measure of our acts,[5] its primary principle in man is identifiable with reason. On the one hand, reason can only make its practical dimension effective through the will, since without the dynamics of the will, reason

---

[3] *Ibid.*, Réponse: « Or, parmi tous les êtres, la créature raisonnable est soumise à la providence divine d'une manière plus excellente par le fait qu'elle participe elle-même de cette providence à pourvoyant à soi-même et aux autres. »

[4] *Ibid.*, Q. 90, art. 4.

[5] *Ibid.*, art. 1.

could not provide itself with the means to achieve the desired end; on the other hand, the will, if it is not to err, must be regulated by reason. Nonetheless, the command of reason is a necessary but not sufficient condition for the law to be fully effective; this command must have a universal and not a particular end. This means that, as a "prescription of practical reason,"[6] it determines what we should do and what we should abstain from (the precept at the basis of all the other precepts of natural law),[7] the light of our natural reason enabling us to discern precisely with natural law what is right and what is wrong. There is therefore an end common to all acts, which, as a first principle, assigns its raison d'être to the choices of practical reason. Even if practical reason, by virtue of its object - human action marked by its particularity and contingency - does not possess the infallibility enjoyed by the demonstrative conclusions of the sciences through theoretical reason, it does remind us that acting rationally implies that a being strives to attain its

[6] *Ibid.*, Q. 91, art. 3.

[7] *Ibid.*, Q. 94, art. 2.

own good; and this good, considered beyond its particular goal, is identifiable with the supreme good understood as beatitude. Consequently, and this applies to both the ethical and political orders, law constitutes the rule of action directed towards happiness. From then on, human law can only have as its goal the realization of the good that underlies and exceeds the good of individuals, i.e., the common or collective good.

Political existence has meaning and value only if man, as a reasonable creature, understands what the eternal law imperatively commands him to do. The immanence of this presence within us translates immediately and concretely into an inclination towards certain ends corresponding to our nature, which makes us what we are. There is a refraction in each individual of the eternal law, immanent to our nature, which is none other than natural law. The prescriptions of the latter are articulated to the sphere of natural inclinations. Man is thereby referred to an onto-ethical principle: practical reason makes the good the first knowable in the order of practice, just as being is the first knowable in the order of theoretical reason.[8] Natural law presupposes an axiom that is self-evident to practical reason, yet unprovable: that the good is the object of a universal desire, and that an action is performed as a function of an end that is the good. This is why there can be no other founding precept for such a law than the following: it is imperative to seek and realize the good, and to abstain from evil. From this follow the other precepts of natural law, which amount to a participation in human good. Indeed, the ordering of the precepts of natural law is modeled on the ordering of natural inclinations, as revealed by the fact that every living thing moves and acts under the impulse of its desires and aversions. As "every substance seeks the preservation of its own being,"[9] what is first in man corresponds to the inclination towards what is good according to his nature. Natural law is, therefore, inherent in the very essence of living beings (and, in man's case, of living beings endowed with reason), and makes intelligible what lies at the root of their actions. It re-

[8] *Ibid.*

[9] *Ibid.*

veals that man, like all living beings, desires the preservation of his being and that which ensures its duration, such as the integrity of his person or his health. There is therefore an ontological requirement that man cannot escape: the tendency to persevere in his being, or the act by which he makes himself being by continuing to be. This tendency is understood as exclusion from the duration of non-being. Being is inseparable from its affirmation; through it, it contributes to the production of its own raison d'être. The second precept concerns the inclination specific to the nature common to the animal kingdom: to reproduce, to care for one's offspring.[10] According to the third precept, man is inclined to seek what is good in accordance with the principles of reason. Thus, it is up to man to coexist with his fellow creatures to overcome his natural deficiencies, to produce truth through science, to avoid the servitude of ignorance, and to seek the truth about God.

Nevertheless, the universality of natural law, immanent in human nature, cannot mask the diffi-

---

[10] *Ibid.*

culty posed by the diversity of human law, arising from the particularity and contingency of action. How can we reconcile these universal principles with the concrete nature of political practice and its application? Human nature provides man with the instruments to respond to the political problem; however, it is up to human law to actualize within the limits of practical reason what cannot be imposed by itself as the exercise of virtue in politics. This is the function of constraint and sanction for those who reject the principles of natural law, and to guarantee their fellow human beings a peaceful life,[11] because the power of reason can also be instrumentalized to satisfy greed or the desire to dominate one's fellow human beings.

It is from this heritage that Suarez and Locke problematize and reshape Thomas Aquinas's legacy of the law of nature. The natural condition of men, as they see it - and which can only be accounted for by reference to the law of nature - is marked by their equality and the reciprocity of their relations, implying that all forms of subordination or subjection

---

[11] *Ibid.*, Q. 95, art. 1.

are ignored, with no one having the right to restrict the behavior of his fellow men. By the same token, it presents freedom as the condition and means of a fulfilled existence in its humanity. For Locke, to be free for each individual means, from the moment when reason must be the guiding principle in all things, to be the rule of his actions, and this in an autonomous way, and, consequently, the individual disposes of his goods (his life, his body, and his possessions) as he deems beneficial to himself. Nevertheless, this freedom, "uncontrollable to dispose of his person or possessions, yet he has not liberty to destroy himself,"[12] is not unrestrained; it does not express a state of license,[13] and, although not political, it is not amoral. This implies that freedom is inconceivable without law. Indeed, man is "capable of law"[14] and "creatures beings, capable of laws, where there is no law there is no freedom."[15]

---

[12] J. LOCKE, *Two treatises of government*, Book II, Ch. II, n. 6, p. 119.

[13] *Ibid.*

[14] J. LOCKE, *An essay concerning human understanding*, Book II, Ch. XXVII, § 26, p. 346.

[15] J. LOCKE, *Two treatises of government*, Book II, n.

And at the foundation of all law, and the condition for determining its value, is the law of nature, which can be likened to a divine and rational law, universally binding on mankind[16] because it imposes itself as a rule and a measure of the general good of humanity.[17] It is signified to them "by the light of nature or by way of Revelation;"[18] it possesses a value before the institution of any positive law, and is the object of a knowledge possible by means of natural human faculties alone.[19] The law of nature,

---

57, p. 143.

[16] *Ibid.*, n. 135, p. 185: « Thus the law of Nature stands as an eternal rule to all men, legislators as well as others. »

[17] J. LOCKE, *An essay concerning human understanding*, Book II, Ch. XXVIII, § 8, p. 352, and § 11, p. 354–356.

[18] *Ibid.*

[19] J. LOCKE, *Essais sur la loi de nature*, Essai VI, p. 107 :" Cette loi contient tout ce que requiert l'obligation envers une loi. En effet, Dieu, l'auteur de cette loi, a voulu qu'elle soit la règle de nos mœurs et de notre vie, et l'a fait promulguer suffisamment pour que n'importe qui, s'il veut bien y consacrer son étude et son activité, et tourner son esprit vers la connaissance de cette loi, puisse la connaître. »

which is both divine and rational (since reason is not its author, although it is its interpreter),[20] constitutes the onto-ethical foundation for the use of practical reason, as an obligation that imposes itself and its commandments on man as soon as he becomes aware of his being and begins his experience of existence. This beginning is to be articulated with the axiom that "all living beings are subject to its authority (divine will) and contain within them their own laws of generation and life."[21] The question underlying the law-of-nature position is: to what extent is it conceivable to define man in relation to the entire kingdom of living things as the only being in the universe alien to any law "without intention, without rule, without a norm that orders his life."[22] That there should be laws for everything that exists, without there being any for man, who is the only one to perceive these same laws, and through which he would have a rule presiding over the orientation of his being, would mean for him

---

[20] *Ibid.*, Essai I, p. 7.

[21] *Ibid.*, p. 3.

[22] *Ibid.*

that his reason would be without reason, and the value of his practice without foundation. From this perspective, the function of reason is not to found the law of nature, but to reveal it to himself as the expression of a higher will present in every consciousness, i.e., the moment of revelation of a transcendence in immanence, or of an immanence that can only be a call to the transcendence that founds it. The result, according to this theological-political orientation, is that positive laws in society are not foundational because they are not binding in themselves; they achieve this claim only by reference to the law of nature, whose command to obey a higher authority responds to the imperative of maintaining public peace.[23] It is possible to compel the human multitude to obey by force, not by obligation.

For both Suarez and Locke, therefore, it is a moral rule binding every individual within himself. Such a law is known by natural light, thus dispensing with the need for revelation. Nevertheless, in Locke's view, it does not refer to any innate idea, for "no principle, whether practical or speculative, is by

---

[23] *Ibid.*, p. 17.

nature inscribed in the souls of men."[24] It must be concluded that reason can only access it through sensible experience, and that such a law is alien to human consent, even though it is the starting point for the legitimacy of all consent. In this sense, it binds men together by imposing obligations, which is tantamount to recognizing that there is no obligation to be obliged, but rather the other of obligation: constraint that makes it possible. This would be explained by the possibility for men to intentionally deny or ignore what is constitutive of their humanity. This signifies the ever-present gap between the interests of each individual and the law of nature's universality and transhistoricity.[25] In this sense, the latter position is inseparable from the thesis that, for both authors, the world is not left to chance or to the absence of finality.[26] Whether we consider the natural given or relations between men, they can only become intelligible through reason. The result

---

[24] *Ibid.*, Essai III, p. 51.

[25] *Ibid.*, Essai VII, p. 117: « L'obligation envers la loi ne change jamais, bien que le temps et les circonstances de l'action changent souvent. »

[26] *Ibid.*, Essai IV, p. 55.

is an identity between the law of nature and reason[27] as a universal law, which is tantamount to recognizing that the law of nature constitutes an intelligible fact in itself, capable of being self-evident to a being endowed with reason. Nevertheless, if primary experience proves sufficient to understand what natural law is, it is also self-evident in its necessity, since reason gains access to it "through reality derived from the senses."[28] Not only is man endowed with faculties that he must exercise, since the Creator wants him to act and not live in idleness and laziness,[29] but it is up to him to fulfill his humanity, to do what he is naturally inclined to do when he "discovers in himself the senses and reason."[30] Thus, because the law of nature makes everyone see that he is equal to his fellow man, it is clear to him that

---

[27] *Ibid.*, p. 67: « Il existe un grand architecte de toute cette création, dont il faut reconnaître la puissance, mais aussi la sagesse ; il s'ensuit qu'il n'a pas créé ce monde en vain et à la légère ; car il est contraire à tant de sagesse de travailler sans un but déterminé. »

[28] *Ibid.*, p. 53.

[29] *Ibid.*, p. 67.

[30] *Ibid.*

no one is legitimately in a position to harm another, to threaten his life, his health, his freedom or his property.[31] By the same token, in view of the weakness of his initial condition, he no longer seeks to coexist with his fellow human beings, but to provide himself with the means to live together sustainably, for "love and want of society, no sooner brought any number of them together, but they presently united and incorporated it, they designed to continue together."[32] From this foundational experience, the raison d'être of political society is to build and preserve a common life to meet the needs of humankind and for its own benefit; this is because man is driven by his propensity to be part of a society and to preserve it as his own, through language, technology, and work. As a result, the law of nature imposes itself as a divine command, a rule of reason, and the very structure of human nature. It is the foundation of the theological-political constitution, establishing its onto-ethical consequences: it

---

[31] J. LOCKE, *Two treatises of government*, Book II, Ch. II, n. 6, p. 119.

[32] *Ibid.*, n. 101, p. 166.

assigns a raison d'être to human practice by orienting it universally, and it condenses the universal commandments of humankind by focusing reason on its practical dimension: man's duty towards the Creator, towards his neighbor, and towards himself.[33] Transgression of these duties, which is contrary to the peace and preservation of the human race, can only result in the punishment of the entire community.

Because man alone has the capacity to access the divine by conceiving the existence of the Creator, the law of nature assigns a sense of being and purpose to the presence of reason within him. It has a divine foundation and is inseparable from the world's teleologically oriented order. It is through this law that we are led towards the best, for it constitutes a standard of moral rectitude, a condition of possibility for the existence of all knowledge of good and evil, as Cicero[34] reminded us. In its absence, no

---

[33] J. LOCKE, *Essais sur la loi de nature*, Essai IV, p. 71.

[34] CICERON, *Des lois*, Paris, Garnier-Flammarion, 1965, traduction par Ch. Appuhn, Livre I, Ch. XV, p.

preservation of humanity is conceivable,[35] and anything opposed to it would be null and void;[36] its abolition would lead to the destruction of the state, authority, and order.[37] And injustice and violence simply express a refusal or lack of obedience to the law of nature, and therefore a practice prejudicial to reason, equity, and the value of the individual. At the same time, man acknowledges his total responsibility in directing his mode of existence, since every individual in the state of nature is the actor of his natural rights. Finally, through its ethical dimen-

---

141–142. Et dans ce même volume, *De la république*, Livre III, Ch. XXII, p. 88.

[35] J. LOCKE, *Essais sur la loi de nature*, Essai VI, p. 109 :" Cette loi est la volonté de ce législateur tout-puissant et nous la connaissons grâce à la lumière et aux principes naturels ; sa connaissance ne peut être cachée à personne, à moins d'aimer l'aveuglement et l'obscurité et de renier la nature pour fuir son devoir. »

[36] J. LOCKE, *Two Treatises of Government*, Book II, n. 135, p. 185: « (...) the fundamental law of Nature being the preservation of mankind, no human sanction can be good or valid against it. »

[37] J. LOCKE, *Essais sur la loi de nature*, Essai VI, p. 109.

sion, the law of nature politically constitutes peace as the specific end of the human condition.

This is why the law of nature makes social existence possible, starting from the initial situation of the state of nature, by guaranteeing the legitimacy of powers and the respect for the resulting conventions.[38] Theoretically, human beings would be able to coexist in a state of peace and mutual preservation in accordance with reason if each individual were to set himself up as the guarantor of the law of nature. The latter would in this sense have a sufficient power of obligation inseparable from the position of a natural sociability of men; "for every obligation binds the conscience and imposes a bond on the soul itself, to the point that it is not the fear of punishment but the reason of righteousness that

---

[38] *Ibid.*, Essai I, p. 15:" (...) Sans cette loi, les hommes ne peuvent avoir aucune relation sociale ni union entre eux. C'est que la société des hommes repose manifestement sur deux fondements : une constitution définie de la société civile accompagnée de la forme du gouvernement et de la garantie des contrats ; si on les abolit, toute communauté humaine s'effondre ; si on abolit la loi de nature, ces principes s'effondreront aussi. »

obliges us."[39] Nevertheless, there is a political society because the force of obligation is not enough, and this is due to human weakness[40] and fragility, which have subjected man to both theoretical and practical wandering, accentuated by submission to the passions; or it has force only through the force of penal sanctions, by which those who do not recognize the obligatory force of legislative power for the conduct of their lives, "acknowledge their submission to this power by experiencing its force, which they would like not to follow."[41] Such is the law of nature that it encompasses all that is required by obligation to the law. Because the Creator is the author of this law, and it expresses His will that it should be the guiding principle of our ways of being and of our existence (respect and fear of divinity, filial piety, love of neighbor...)[42] He "has had it promulgated sufficiently so that anyone, if he is willing to devote his study

---

[39] *Ibid.*, Essai VI, p. 103.

[40] J. LOCKE, *Two treatises of government*, Book II, Ch. XII, n. 143, p. 190–191.

[41] J. LOCKE, *Essais sur la loi de nature*, Essai VI, p. 103.

[42] *Ibid.*, Essai VIII, p. 119.

to it, and turn his mind to the knowledge of this law, can know it."[43] The theological and political axiom that follows from this is as follows: the basis of the legislators' authority over other men, their legitimacy to demand obedience and to compel obedience, they derive from the Creator, for it is of the essence of the law of nature that He promulgates to universally and originally bind all men. And if man distinguishes himself from other creatures, it is precisely because he possesses the power to rectify and perfect himself by appearing to himself to be responsible for what he is.

This theological-political problematic is common to the Suarezian position on natural law. From a theological perspective, it invites us to consider man "from the point of view of a double nature and a double light of reason."[44] It is possible to see man in accordance with his pure nature, thinking and acting by means of the light of reason, or according to the specificity of grace transmitted by divine light, which orients him according to his situation

---

[43] *Ibid.*, Essai VI, p. 107.

[44] SUAREZ, *Des lois*, I, 3, n. 12, p. 10.

as a finite being or "traveler." There is, therefore, a dual rational law: 1°) one natural to man, 2°) the other supernatural to grace, which, however, can be qualified as natural because it guides men here below and enlightens them in their choice of existence. If the essence of law lies in natural law, the latter is also the foundation of all human rights.

Consequently, the development of this concept in relation to the legacy of tradition must respond to a primary imperative: how can its status and practical effectiveness be made explicit without, contrary to the Stoic tradition, for example, subjecting human nature to the passivity of participation in the order of the world, and conceiving man as responsible before God for what he does with his life? It's a question of removing natural law from an ontological order that is both the measure of reason and the essence of man, and constituting it as the manifestation of an ethical norm immanent to finite being.[45]

---

[45] *Ibid.*, II, 5, n. 12, p. 103: «Natural law is given in man, not in God, since it is temporal and created. It is not given externally to man, for it is not written on tablets but in hearts. »

This presupposes the removal of an equivocation: rational nature itself constitutes an essence, not a law, since it must be remembered that nature as such does not command, does not reveal moral good or evil, does not direct or enlighten, and consequently does not produce any effect proper to law; this is why nature cannot be qualified as law except metaphorically. Thus, rational nature alone, which would act as the measure or foundation of moral goodness, is not a sufficient condition for the generation of law, and therefore, strictly speaking, cannot be called natural law. According to Suarez, it is imperative to distinguish between two aspects of rational nature: nature itself, as the basis for the agreement or disagreement of human actions with it, and the ability that nature possesses to discern which of human operations do or do not conform to it; such an ability is called natural reason. From this perspective (corresponding to Suarez's Thomist position), nature constitutes only an indirect foundation of natural goodness, and the rational faculty expresses natural law itself insofar as it commands or forbids the human will to do what is morally right.[46]

Natural law thus reveals the basis of an ethic independent of submission to a cosmological structure, and of a theologization of the Stoic *Logos* as divine rationality. Earlier, Plato equated natural law with "every natural inclination placed in things by their creator, through which each of them tends towards its own acts and ends."[47] For Suarez, this heritage calls for a correction in the use of words. The term law is legitimately applicable to things only metaphorically. Animals, for example, are not capable of it, as they have neither reason nor freedom. Consequently, natural law, strictly considered "as the participation of the eternal law in the rational creature,"[48] is of the order of moral science and theology, because only man can establish a link between action and the value of the end. It is called natural 1°) to differentiate it from the supernatu-

---

[46] *Ibid.*, n. 9, p. 102.

[47] *Ibid.*, I, 3, n. 8, p. 9.

[48] THOMAS D'AQUIN, *Somme théologique*, I^a–II^{ae}, Q. 91, art. 2.

ral,[49] 2°) because the Creator introduced it into nature; it is thus inseparable from man's rational nature, which enables him to distinguish between good and evil.[50] A metaphysical principle can be superimposed on the political order: if every second cause, by virtue of its finiteness, has a raison d'être only in relation to the infinity of a first cause, then it must be recognized that human law, by taking natural law as its model, is the second cause of the eternal law that men cannot know by itself. Nevertheless, the eternal law is not capable of binding by

---

[49] SUÁREZ, *De Legibus*, I, 3, n. 11, p. 10: « Indeed, it's worth noting that the philosophers did not know man's supernatural end, but only evoked a particular happiness in this life, or better, the right conditions for living in peace and justice, and addressed the theme of laws in relation to this temporal end.»

[50] *Ibid.*, II, 4, n. 9, p. 99: «In the course of their existence, human beings come to know the eternal law through the mediation of its participation and, consequently, by means of just, temporal, and created laws. Just as second causes reveal the first cause, and creatures reveal the Creator, so temporal laws, which participate in eternal law, manifest the source from which they emanate. »

itself, apart from any other law. It requires articulation with a specific law - human law - to compel in deed. According to theological and metaphysical principles, only the eternal law has the obligatory character of a universal cause, whereas in the political order, obligation has human law as its proximate cause. For Suarez, this means that the way in which eternal law obliges is less direct than that of human laws.[51]

As for natural law, it is neither immediately given in man's nature, nor in his will, since it is precisely the human will[52] that depends on it; it is linked to it. Through natural law, the will, by ordering itself at the command of reason, is affirmed as a free act imputable to the agent. In this sense, natural law is not reduced to an indicative judgment of human reason, through which the goodness or badness of an act is revealed. Still, it obliges man to act or not to act in a certain way, as a manifestation of

---

[51] *Ibid.*, n. 10, p. 99.

[52] *Ibid.*, 5, n. 12, p. 103.

the divine will.[53] Natural law is therefore an ethical law whose principle, the light of natural reason, constitutes the supreme condition of morality, for it enables us to determine what conforms with human nature; it resides "in reason as the immediate intrinsic rule of human actions."[54] Consequently, rational nature itself is the foundation of natural goodness, appearing as the very sign of morality. In this sense, natural law is the index of the effectiveness of morality as an affirmation of will and freedom, and no longer as an adaptation to prior knowledge; by the same token, it embodies the moment when the will freely decides to do good. The man who complies with the commandment of right reason "is his own law."[55]

In view of this autonomy of reason in the practical order, Suarez asks what function habitus plays in the efficiency of natural law, so as not to reduce the law to an act whose object is reducible to a guiding

---

[53] *Ibid.*, n. 13, p. 108: «Natural law is a genuine and authentic divine law, for which God is the lawgiver.»

[54] *Ibid.*, 5, n. 12, p. 103.

[55] *Ibid.*, n. 10, p. 102.

rule.[56] Indeed, natural law manifests itself to man in the form of a practical judgment. However, the latter is not in itself capable of making an agent move, except by a free act of the will. Consequently, habitus facilitates the will's movement toward what the understanding sees in two ways. 1°) As a disposition acquired for the purpose of enabling a faculty to do or refrain from doing, habitus predisposes the understanding so that the commands of human nature and their property as law appear to it with the greatest possible clarity. 2°) The *habitus* is an auxiliary enabling the rational appetite to tend towards the commandments of reason, so that the good ordered by practical judgment is desired, or the evil represented is the object of aversion. Since natural law is not, strictly speaking, the object of promulgation, it cannot possess the same power of obligation as positive law. *Habitus* is therefore a condition for man's access to morality and justice, and for his becoming his own law. But it is also a condition without which it would be impossible to understand how natural

---

[56] *Ibid.*, n. 13, p. 103.

law obliges a free will by means of the practical judgment of reason.

It is on this condition that a practical judgment that is not positively promulgated and based on the rectitude of the ordering of practice is able to claim effectiveness. A practical judgment in line with reason acquires by its orientation the force of law, even if it is not written down.[57] According to the Gospels,[58] prior to any positive manifestation of the law, there is a law engraved in the human heart, attested by the conscience, which "testifies whether a man acts wrongly or rightly, when he opposes or follows the natural commandment of right reason."[59] And if such a commandment is equivalent to the natural law signifying the moment when the reasonable being becomes for himself his own law, this is made possible because man carries immanently within himself the foundation of all future law through the mediation of the commandment of natural reason.

---

[57] *Ibid.*, n. 10, p. 102.

[58] *Rom.* 2, 14–15: «Gentiles who have no law fulfill what is by nature the law; even without having a law, they are the law for themselves.»

[59] SUÁREZ, *De Legibus*, II, 5, n. 10, p. 102.

And this immanence is the mark of supreme eminence, for "the natural law is nothing other than a certain natural participation in the eternal law."[60] This is the paradox of the immanence of natural law, which should be self-founding and yet is not self-sufficient insofar as it receives its foundation from a transcendence that exceeds it.

Nevertheless, this immanence remains the anchor of a problematic of free causality, which is precisely what the theme of *habitus* contributes to. Indeed, through the mediation of *habitus*, rational faculties make it possible to extend the domain of human operations, i.e., to make it easier to work towards one's goals. It is specific to human acts to leave their mark on the rational faculties in the manner of *habitus*. And the human will has the power to direct itself towards the fulfillment of an obligation expressed by a practical judgment of reason; it thereby manifests a free causality. With regard to the *habitus*, it appears that the will disposes itself to respect the obligations commanded by reason, thus translating the moment when the faculties

---

[60] *Ibid.*

and the *habitus* concur in the accomplishment of an act in conformity with natural law.

In the light of these considerations, and of the analyses of freedom developed in *Metaphysical Dispute XIX*, it appears that natural law can only claim to express an ethical and political dimension as a function of the founding division made between causes that act necessarily[61] and those that act freely and contingently.[62] If natural law is only conceivable in conformity with reason, this in turn means that causes that act without reason necessarily act. Suarez, like Locke, uses the question of natural law to establish an intrinsic link between freedom and rationality. Thus, man's sensory appetite expresses no faculty or power to act freely, since such an appetite is alien to reason. Man is an efficient cause acting according to a free mode of being, each individually or collectively experiencing such an active power said to be free by its power and intrinsic nature. In this sense, freedom emerges from reason, for only

---

[61] SUÁREZ, *O. O.*, vol. 25, *D. M. XIX*, Section I, pp. 688–693.

[62] *Ibid.*, Section II, p. 693–700.

the intellect is capable of expressing an intention, of assigning meaning to the ends sought, of thinking and implementing the appropriate means to achieve them, and thus of deliberating. Only an active faculty or power is free, since it alone is capable of moving from one state to another, unlike a purely passive faculty,[63] as Locke confirms following Suarez. In this sense, the commandment of natural law confirms, through the very possibility of complying with it or not, that man acts freely at the moment he performs his action, independently of what he had previously wished to accomplish. It is from this problematic framework that Suarez and Locke will formulate the question of the foundation of political power and civil law.

---

[63] Voir J. LOCKE, *An Essay Concerning Human Understanding*, Book II, Ch. XXI, § 2, p. 234.

III

Freedom, the Raison d'être of Politics. The Ethical Foundation of Politics and the Political Actualization of Ethics

In the Suarezian analysis, the primacy of reason implies not only the search for efficiency in action, through the requirement of conformity of means to ends, but also its moral foundation, insofar as the content of the law is identified with an upright and honest rule, the measure of action,[1] Nevertheless, in the use of practical reason, the intellect does not have the power to directly move the will, which is defined precisely by freedom. What is represented by the intellect cannot lay claim to such efficiency, since the very nature of the will is that it "arises

[1] SUÁREZ, *De Legibus,* I, 3, n. 19, p. 12.

freely in act."[2] When the will acts, it does so freely, just as when it does not act, because at the moment it acts, it might not do so. It will freely determine itself by bringing about the act.[3] The function of the intellect, on the other hand, is purely one of orientation, once the voluntary act has been directed towards a given object, and consists in determining the appropriate means to achieve it, since it is specific to the will to tend first towards ends. According to Suarez, the will is an absolutely free power, the only one capable of determining itself towards an object. On the one hand, the intellect grasps the nature of good and evil, and evaluates whether or not it is appropriate to move towards what is legitimate; on the other, the appetite, which is linked to such an evaluation, will be able to desire known goods according to what makes them desirable, and to do so in a free manner. Through knowledge, the appetitive faculty rises, reaches a higher degree, and

---

[2] SUÁREZ, *De Anima*, Introducción y edición crítica por Salvador Castellote, T.3 (Disp. VIII– XIV), Fundación X. Zubiri, Madrid, 1991, Disp. X, Q. 3, n. 6, p. 306.

[3] *Ibid.*, Disp. XII, Q. 2, n. 16, p. 404.

becomes free. Thus, the will, insofar as it is linked to the rational and discursive faculty, is free, because free will derives from the intellect and reason.[4] Between the will and free will, there is a real identity and reason. This gives rise to a double denomination: we speak of will when there is a movement towards an end, and which is the cause of volitions; we speak of free will when the will, by its free choice, sets as its objects the means intended to achieve its goal.

But what are the objects for which it is legitimate to speak of free will? To answer this question, we need to distinguish between two types of will:[5] the "exercising will," which involves the possibility of starting or stopping an act, and the "specifying will," which consists of the possibility of performing an act or its opposite, such as loving or hating. Hence, if the will is generally directed towards good or happiness, it is so only from the point of view of its specification, not its exercise, which confirms the necessity of the law and its accompanying sanction.

---

[4] *Ibid.*, n. 11, p. 398.
[5] *Ibid.*, n. 13, p. 400.

Suarez's argument is based on the following postulates. 1°) Since happiness and goodness do not present any form of evil, it does not seem possible to reject them and make them objects of aversion. 2°) The fact remains, however, that such is the existence of the finite, reasonable creature that the love of goodness and happiness does not impose itself on him as necessary, and that, consequently, his will is not necessarily compelled to realize them. This is because no good in this life does not also entail evils and difficulties. From this point of view, there is a distortion between the will and the intellect, the latter not being free in its exercise and remaining dependent on the influence of the will. Nevertheless, from the point of view of specification, the intellect is necessarily compelled to assent if what it aims at appears in its truth with clarity and evidence, as is the case, for example, in geometry and calculation. As for the will, as human experience establishes, it does not necessarily feel compelled to love, even if this appears to it with the evidence of its goodness; this is also why it is possible to go against the commands of natural law. This is illustrated by the discrepancy between the nature of the object of theoretical reason and that of the object of practical reason. In the order of theoretical reason, truth imposes itself by its uniqueness, since if what is stated is proven, it excludes all error (if there is conformity to the principle of identity or non-contradiction, for example), whereas in the order of practical reason, good can exist in association with elements of evil, as confirmed in social life by the need for constraint and punishment if there is to be respect for law and justice.

The political stakes of the law must therefore be interpreted in terms of the problematic balance sought between the function of the will and that of the intellect. On the one hand, the absolute freedom of the will cannot ignore the decisive role of the rational content that must accompany it. To establish a practical determination as a law, a measure is required, that of the production of a right judgment concerning the appropriate means to the end sought. But the intellect also expresses its freedom by evaluating and comparing the properties of the objects of the will, which amounts to recognizing that the freedom of the will derives for its effective fulfillment from the intellect. The intellect not only delimits the proper use of freedom of will (knowing why we choose what we choose, thereby establishing the possibility of attributing our own choices to ourselves and making us responsible for our will), but also constitutes the indefiniteness of its perspectives in a space that is both rationally determined and commensurate with man, because it reduces indeterminacy to a minimum. The intellect must ensure that the freedom of the will does not escape our nature, that it asserts itself as a positive and responsible power of choice, i.e., that it does not turn into its opposite, servitude, or deny itself in the will of evil for evil's sake.

On the other hand, the essence of law is not reducible to reference to a practical judgment expressing a content consistent with the specific end of human nature. Still, for there to be law, reference must also be made to the will of a superior with the power to assert and impose this judgment on subjects, manifesting the intention to compel its fulfillment effectively. According to Thomas Aquinas's definition of law, which is one of the starting points of Suarezian thought, it is identifiable as "an ordinance of reason for the common good, promulgated by the one in charge of the community."[6] For Suarez, the ambiguity of this determination lies in the formula "ordinance of reason," which must be understood in an active rather than passive sense.[7] The active prescription is produced by the legislator, while having reason as its origin. Yet it must be attributed to both the intellect and the will, for it is legitimate to argue that the latter expresses a rational power, just as it is relevant to say that it is enunciated by reason.

Nonetheless, the law emanates from a superior "with power and responsibility over his subjects."[8] And for an ordinance to be effective, it must be able to be accompanied by coercive force - something that reason does not inherently possess, and which is precisely what leads to the differentiation between advice and law. In this sense, for Suárez, the law is promulgated with the precise aim of establishing a

---

[6] THOMAS D'AQUIN, *Somme théologique*, I^{a}–II^{ae}, Q. 90, art. 4.

[7] SUÁREZ, *De Legibus*, I, 12, n. 3, p. 53.

[8] *Ibid.*, n. 4, p. 53.

stable and lasting obligation[9] whose foundation is not so much the ordinance of reason aimed at the common good as the command of the will backed by a binding force, without which respect for natural law would be no more than a fiction. An analogy between metaphysical and juridico-political concepts can be drawn from these remarks: just as existence is the being-in-act of an essence, which confers effectivity, the ordinance of reason achieves effectivity only through a command of the will of a superior possessing coercive power. If reason is the essence of the law, the will, the sign of action and power, it consecrates its effectivity. Politically, reason does not constitute a power to act in and of itself; it is the power of the superior that establishes its performative efficacy. For the precept laid down by the law to be general, just, and stable, it must conform to reason insofar as it makes possible the rectitude of practical judgment and its recognition. And the obligatory character of the law is insepara-

---

[9] *Ibid.*, n. 5, p. 53: «We could, perhaps, propose the following, shorter definition: law is a general, just and stable precept, promulgated as appropriate.»

ble from a will that clearly and distinctly promulgates it, notably by relying on *habitus,* making it possible for the subject to accept its command. However, natural law, as the *habitus* of moral principles in this understanding of law, has a specific status for which intellectual determination[10] is decisive, since it is the only way of "discerning the honest from the unworthy,"[11] which is why it forms part of moral science and theology. The man who orients himself by means of this commandment of practical reason becomes his own law, i.e., the primary representation is converted into an effective operation. As a result, the *habitus* of the practical intellect elevates reason to an ever clearer and more distinct knowledge of the natural law through the mediation of synderesis. In contrast, the *habitus* of the will contributes to man's perfection in the fulfillment of a type of existence in conformity with

---

[10] *Ibid.*, II, 5, n. 14, p. 103:" (…) Natural law consists of a judgment made by the mind. I would add, by the same token, that the natural light of the intellect, prompt in itself to dictate what we should do, can also be called natural law. »

[11] *Ibid.*, I, 3, n. 10, p. 9.

the natural law. Nevertheless, it remains the condition of possibility of the morality of every will, indissociable from obligation in conscience. It reminds us that we do not choose to be morally free, without which there would be no possible foundation for the value of action. In this way, rational nature forms the basis of natural goodness without imposing an obligation and, at the same time, asserts itself as a criterion of morality.

At the foundation of the legitimacy of civil law, therefore, is natural law,[12] a commandment of reason, requiring voluntary obedience, showing that obedience does not originate solely from force.[13] Ideally, natural law should lead to voluntary obedience, indicating that when apprehended, there is no other legitimate response than to do what it commands. Every law posits obligation as the guiding principle and justification for action. Ultimately, the law's obligation manifests a type of necessity imposed on the practical order, by means of which the

---

[12] *Ibid.*, II, 6, n. 1, p. 104: «Natural law dictates what is right or wrong, independently of any superior will.»

[13] *Ibid.*, 10, n. 4, p. 123.

intellect orients the will; it has a demonstrative and preceptive dimension. The very nature of law is to command and enable the government of man by man; it therefore exists to guide action, and thus has a heuristic function in revealing what is good or bad for a rational nature.[14] It also has a preceptive function, since as an expression of a superior's will, "it causes movement and creates an impulse,"[15] i.e., it causes action to be taken, and if necessary, by constraint. The legislator's ability to enact any law, therefore, requires, inseparably, the use of will and intellect. Consequently, knowledge of good and evil is not enough to constitute a law; power is needed to compel and, possibly, impose an obligation to act in a certain way to preserve humanity. From then on, we cannot separate the ethical character of law from its political condition of possibility. It is based on this agreement-discordance and its legacy that Locke's creation and purpose of civil societies must also be analyzed, to propose a theory of government

---

[14] *Ibid.*, n. 3, p. 122.

[15] *Ibid.*, I, 4, n. 7, p. 15.

exercising limited powers and based on the consent of the governed.

According to this perspective, man's weakness and finitude have led him, in the course of his history (slavery, conquests, tyranny, and usurpation), to adopt unnatural behavior, substituting force and arbitrariness for the law of nature. For man to comply with the ethical law of obligation constituted by the law of nature immanent to human reason, it is up to him - to use a Kantian formula - to "obstruct that which obstructs"[16] his natural rights, i.e., to ensure through political power the rights inherent in the human person through peace and security. Like the Suarezian analysis, the development of this reflection takes as its starting point a questioning of the nature of the relationship between the understanding and the will, considered as powers of the mind,[17] to clarify the mode of being free. In reality,

---

[16] Kant, E., *Métaphysique des mœurs. Première partie. Doctrine du droit, Introduction à la doctrine du droit*, Paris, Vrin, 1971, traduction A. Philonenko, § D, p. 105.

[17] J. LOCKE, *An essay concerning human understanding*, Book II, Ch. XXI, § 5, p. 236.

there are two types of power, one active and the other passive.[18] This division does not mean that matter is reduced to a passive power, and therefore, devoid of any active power. Still, it does enable us to grasp man's mode of being as susceptible to both active and passive power. And power implies a type of relation to action or change.[19] Nevertheless, if we consider bodies, they are not in themselves capable of representing the power to initiate action. Only the mind acquires the idea of power from reflection on the workings of its own interiority,[20] either from changes experienced as resulting from the impression of external objects, or from those experienced as consequences of its own determination.

This is why the clearest idea of active power comes from the spiritual order (to move and to

---

[18] *Ibid.*, § 2, p. 234.

[19] *Ibid.*, § 3, p. 234.

[20] *Ibid.*, § 5, p. 236: « This at least I think evident, That we find in ourselves a *Power* to begin or forbear, continue or end several actions of our minds, and motions of our Bodies, barely by a thought or preference of the mind ordering, or as it were commanding the doing or not doing such or such a particular action. »

think),[21] or from thought thinking itself, which clearly shows that we can thereby move the parts of our body when we wish.[22] From then on, man understands himself through this power to begin to act or to refrain from doing so; there is therefore, as for Suarez, a power of the human soul over its actions, through which we acquire the representation of necessity and freedom.[23] Thus, according to Suarez, freedom is identified with the power to act, not with the power to act or to act in a contrary manner. The experience of self-determination by each human being is given at the very moment of decision; it is the proof of the existence of freedom. Only the rational agent is capable of freedom, as long as he is not subject to necessity.[24] In most of his actions, man is not driven by necessity, but by the freedom of his will.[25] The experience of freedom is therefore inherent to our mode of being. For each of us, to

---

[21] *Ibid.*, § 8, p. 237.

[22] *Ibid.*, § 4, p. 234-235.

[23] *Ibid.*, § 7, p. 237.

[24] SUÁREZ, volume 25, *D. M. XIX*, 5, n. 1, p. 711.

[25] *Ibid.*, 2, n. 12, p. 696.

exist is to experience the power to will or not to will, to do or not to do. The faculty of being free can only be active within us, and it is this activity that specifies the free faculty. In this sense, the experience of freedom corresponds to the moment of active exteriorization of the essence of reasonable being. And the use of reason expresses in man the immanence of the free mode of being, the latter finding its full meaning in conformity to reason, which establishes the imputability of action. For both Suarez and Locke, freedom is the condition of possibility of obligation; it calls for it and actualizes this call through law, and the only law to which a free being must conform to preserve his being and develop his nature corresponds to a law of obligation.

And in this perspective of articulation between the understanding and the will, according to Locke, "so far as a Man has a power to think, or not to think; to move, or not to move, according to the preference or direction of his own mind, so far is a Man *Free*."[26] In the exercise of freedom, man under-

---

[26] J. LOCKE, *An essay concerning human understanding*, Book II, Ch. XXI, § 8, p. 237.

stands himself as an agent based on the power he manifests to do or not to do according to the determination of his mind, which reason illuminates and makes possible.[27] In the absence of the possibility of the power to accomplish one of the determinations of the will, there is no freedom, only an agent subject to necessity. Indeed, self-determination is inconceivable outside the mind, the will, and without reference to a volition, i.e., without "actual determination of one's will."[28] Nevertheless, where freedom is absent, there can be thought, will, or volition. If we consider bodies, because their conditions of existence strictly determine them and because they have no thought and volition, we cannot identify them with free agents. And if man is not free about

---

[27] J. LOCKE, *Quelques pensées sur l'éducation*, Paris, Vrin, 1992, traduction de G. Compayré, section XVI, § 122, p. 167 :" (...) l'exercice de la raison est la perfection la plus haute que l'homme puisse atteindre dans la vie. »

[28] J. LOCKE, *An essay concerning human understanding*, Book II, Ch. XXI, § 8, p. 237-238: « (...) where either of the mis not in the Power of the Agent to be produced by him according to his volition. »

the action of willing,[29] it must be recognized that will is the rational dimension of the free act as the result of deliberation, and is thus opposed to the involuntary.[30] As for freedom, as the power to do or not to do what has previously been the subject of deliberation, it expresses the voluntary dimension of the act and is thus opposed to necessity. An example of this is the tennis ball, or a man determined by his reflexes and acting "by Necessity and Constraint,"[31] or for whom, in view of the physiological process, it is obviously impossible to make his heart beat or not. Freedom is a constitutive idea of a person having "the power of doing, or forbearing to do."[32] From then on, our representation of freedom is limited to the scope of such power. For anything that impedes this power, or hinders its possibility of contrary orientation, denies freedom.[33] Every free agent

---

[29] *Ibid.*, § 22, p. 244-245.

[30] *Ibid.*, § 11, p. 239.

[31] *Ibid.*, § 9, p. 238.

[32] *Ibid.*, § 10, p. 238.

[33] *Ibid.*, § 12, p. 239:" As it is in the motions of the Body, so it is in the Thoughts of our Minds; where any one is such, that we have power to take it up, or lay it by,

expresses through his mind a power to begin or cease his bodily movements and thoughts according to what he deems, after deliberation, to conform with his choices. We speak of necessity when thought is absent, i.e., when there is no power to act or not to act based on a chosen orientation of the mind,[34] i.e., a preference that the mind gives to one or the other.

Will and freedom as faculties of action constitute, in this perspective, two distinct powers of the agent.[35] The intellect and the will, as in Suarez, are constitutive of every free act; the deliberation of the intellect that accompanies it anticipates and prepares the choice; freedom is thus understood as the faculty of acting or not acting. According to Suarez, if the intellect is identified with the power to think

---

according to the preference of the Mind, there we are *at liberty.*»

[34] *Ibid.*, § 27, p. 247:" It is carefully to be remembered, that Freedom consists in the dependence of the Existence, or non-existence *of any Action, upon our Volition of it, and not in the dependence of any Action, or its contrary, on our preference.* »

[35] *Ibid.*, § 16, p. 241.

for oneself, freedom corresponds analogously to the power to begin and act for oneself. It is inseparable from the construction of man's human becoming, since it enables him to think of himself as the primary foundation and end of his actions. As with Locke, society emerges at the heart of a set of obligations that are always already present, given man's nature as a reasonable, free, and finite being with duties laid down by natural law, which is both immanent to his being and driven by a supernatural end. And if we refer to the order structuring social life, it no longer expresses an order before freedom of will and convention, but exists only as a creation of human freedom. By dissociating the order of nature, expressed in necessary and material causality, from the human order, specific to political society and manifesting rational causality, Suarez and Locke articulate man's humanity in a process of self-creation over time. In this sense, through politics and ethics, the experience of freedom confirms the separation between man and nature. Politics confirms another possible beginning: that produced by man. It was precisely the role of natural law to help us understand the basis of this separation, starting from a human nature that is anything but natural, since it consecrates the emergence of a human order rather than the repetition of a pre-established one. With natural law, man's rootedness in political existence and its realization in history identify freedom with an order given by reason in the immanence of interiority. It is as if this same natural law ensures the legitimate transition between nature and culture, leading to ethics and politics. In this way, the experience of freedom is also the cultural foundation of our awareness of belonging to humanity. Through the freedom of our will, we each discover that we are essentially human as a beginning in ourselves. Each of us encounters within ourselves the possibility of becoming human and accessing the universal, i.e., of asserting our autonomy as rational beings, our individuality, to act humanely in a human world in the making, and therefore politically organized.

Consequently, freedom rests on the fact that man is endowed with reason, which instructs him on the natural law by which he is obliged to conduct his existence and govern himself. [36] Reason's knowledge of this law is what makes the human exercise of freedom possible, and consecrates it in its effectiveness. As for Suarez, nothing is more specific to natural law than guaranteeing the common good while ensuring peace and security for all. We must therefore move on from a natural condition in which all possess the right and have the obligation to defend natural law by their own means (which for Suarez corresponds to the situation of an imperfect multitude) to the constitution of a social body (a multitude fulfilled according to a moral order)[37] implying the renunciation by individuals of what they personally consider just or unjust, as well as self-defense and vengeance, i.e., the establishment of a legislative and executive power. The body politic is the condition that enables man to achieve reason within himself and in his relations with his fellow human beings, thereby participating in a teleologi-

---

[36] J. LOCKE, *Two treatises of government*, Book II, Ch. VI, n. 59, p. 170-171.

[37] SUAREZ, *De Legibus*, (O. O.) volume 5, Book III, 2, n. 4, p. 181.

cally organized universe. Man can only consent to this if the body politic itself is the work of reason. And if the law of nature, the principle of moral obligation, confirms man's freedom, it is also what makes him appear to himself as a social being, led by his deficiencies and finiteness to form a society with his fellows,[38] responding not just to a utilitarian end, but to a tendency[39] without which he would not be what he is. From this obligation, the source of all obligation, represented by natural law, it is up to man to freely consent to it, as long as he conforms to reason. Indeed, because he is free, man can only legitimately subscribe to a civil power in line with the principles of natural law and producing its effects according to reason, i.e., to preserve natural rights such as equality, security, and personal freedom, or the right to own property, which he cannot be asked to renounce. To renounce them is to deny the basis of any legitimate obligation, and thus to

---

[38] J. LOCKE, *Two treatises of government*, Book II, Ch. VII, n. 77, p. 154-155.

[39] SUAREZ, *De Legibus*, (O. O.) volume 5, Book III, 1, n. 3, p. 176.

refuse to obey natural law, and thereby to renounce the rights that constitute each individual in his or her humanity. Sociability and the humanization of one's individuality lie at the heart of all obligations, and are indissociable in their ethical and political demands. For both Suárez and Locke, the bond between men results from the combination of two moments arising from the interweaving of nature and history: the sociability of natural existence and the political dimension of artificial existence. Artificiality is what enables the fulfillment of naturalness, and naturalness is that without which artificiality would be inconceivable. In view of the individual's original destitution and weakness, socialization is an existential support (there can be no human existence that is not social), and legislative power is a solution (there can be no successful social existence without politics).

For there to be a community or body politic,[40] there must be the consent of those who constitute it,[41] i.e., a universal reciprocal agreement. Only such

---

[40] *Ibid.*, 3, n. 1, p. 182.

[41] J. LOCKE, *Two treatises of government*, Book II, Ch.

an agreement can legitimize the constitution of society as a civil society. For it is on this basis that any other social agreement or consensus becomes relevant, the primary contract being that it is a question of finding the principles of an agreement, the only point on which there can be unanimity, and on which any other agreement can be satisfied with the majority and disregard a universality that is no longer to be found. This is precisely what leads Suarez, for example, to envisage a double type of agreement at the origin of political power, or two types of pact that are equally necessary, whether considered as conditions of possibility or from an ethical point of view. The first, known as a pact of union,[42] makes up the political body corresponding to the perfect community (*corpus mysticum*). In contrast, the second, a pact of subjection, actualizes the specific power of a community when the community has transferred legislative power to an authority (a ruler or an assembly). Consequently,

---

VIII, n. 95, p. 164-165.

[42] SUAREZ, *De Legibus*, (*O. O.*) volume 5, Book III, 2, n. 4, p. 181.

without universal agreement on the composition of a body politic with a moral unity implying subjection to a governing power, we cannot speak of a political society, with men living together, admittedly, but in a disordered fashion, with no reciprocal obligations towards each other, nor towards a power they will necessarily be led to establish.[43] For Locke, the original deprivation of mankind, combined with the misery of corruption and vice as obstacles to what, according to reason, should be the human race's initial existence, forces men to form multiple societies, a prelude to the fragmentation of the human race into a multiplicity of political societies.[44] "He and all the rest of mankind are one community, make up one society distinct from all other creatures."[45] As with Suarez, the unity of the human race constitutes the first of all societies, inseparable

---

[43] *Ibid.*

[44] J. LOCKE, *Two treatises of government*, Book II, Ch. IX, n. 128, p. 181. Et SUÁREZ, *De Legibus*, (*O. O.*) volume 5, Book III, 2, n. 5, p. 181:" It is not necessary for the preservation or well-being of humanity to join together in a single political community.»

[45] *Ibid.*

from the birth of individuals. The origin of political society is not the passage from a scattered multiplicity to an organized civil unity, but the diffraction of the human community into differentiated political bodies. The genesis of political societies implies the juxtaposition of a multiplicity of self-sufficient units, based on the loss of a pre-existing unity,[46] that of the universal society of humankind, which Suarez believes it is the task of international law to recover historically, both theoretically and practically.

For our two authors, the basis of the difference between a political society and any human aggregate (even if the latter is not incompatible with the position of a pre-existing unity of the human race) is that it requires a decision-making process involving all members of the community. This can only presuppose consent to a legislative power, given that, in accordance with the natural condition of men, no one has natural authority over his fellow man. Laws

---

[46] SUÁREZ, *De Legibus*, (*O. O.*) volume 5, Book III, 2, n. 5, p. 181:" Soon after the creation of the world, men began to divide themselves into multiple states, each with its own distinct power. »

must therefore be established, i.e., specific procedures for collective decision-making,[47] which requires integration into a community directed by a temporal power for the public good by a magistrate endowed with the power to promulgate laws and enforce them through collective power. For Locke, the first human power corresponds to his ability to do whatever he deems appropriate to guarantee his own preservation, the safeguarding of his fellow human beings being delegated to society.[48] The latter's purpose is precisely to safeguard himself and his associates, since civil laws necessarily signify for both authors a limitation of freedom as granted by natural law. Natural law is the principle of original human freedom; as freedom is the teleological reason for natural law, natural law is what brings freedom into being as such. Being born free and capable of reason are the same. The second human power is

---

[47] J. LOCKE, *Two treatises of government*, Book II, Ch. XI, n. 134, p. 183: « The first and fundamental positive law of all commonwealths is the establishing of the legislative power, as the first and fundamental natural law which is to govern even the legislative. »

[48] *Ibid.*, Ch. IX, n. 129, p. 181.

also linked to a renunciation: that of vengeance and the power to punish, designed to ensure respect for natural law, which now implies that everyone is in a position to become an auxiliary to the executive power of political society.[49]

Originally, the community was formed to avoid the insecurity that, in Suárez's case, the absence of laws accepted by all, or in Locke's, of a recognized arbitrator with the power to impose his decisions, would necessarily entail. This has no other aim than the common good, namely the security of individuals and the preservation of the peace, without which there can be no prosperity. As a result, political society is not characterized by the implementation of a contract, but rather by the founding decision[50] to be part of a whole ordered by a human power capable of promulgating laws and enforcing them in the interests of the public good, if necessary, using the power of all the members of the community. The result is the constitution of a single body politic

---

[49] *Ibid.*, n. 130, p. 181.

[50] *Ibid.*, Ch. II, n. 14, p. 124.

guided by a single will,[51] and consequently possessing a unified power to act, consecrating the unifying will of the common good and the means to make it effective. For Locke, this presupposes precisely that "the consent of the majority shall not in reason be received as the act of the whole,"[52] since the unanimous consent of individuals remains virtually impossible.

The end of political society is therefore the existence of individuals who are necessarily forced to coexist, and the contingency of its historical forms cannot obscure the necessity that presides over it. It has no raison d'être except as instituted by men for their own benefit, with reference to the guiding norm of natural law, the condition of harmony between the order of the whole, and individual and collective existence. For both Suárez and Locke, the birth of the community stems from the free and rational consent of each individual, who decides to associate with his fellows in a single political body to live in security. By consenting to obey the laws of

[51] *Ibid.*, Ch. VIII, n. 96, p. 165.

[52] *Ibid.*, n. 98, p. 165.

the state that determine the limits imposed on his natural freedom, the individual also consents to another mode of being. In effect, he consents to unconditional obedience within the legislative framework, with no turning back and no possible dispensation, as his natural powers are transferred to the community.[53] However, this mutation has no other objective than the advent and guarantee of a civil liberty that requires the abandonment of the primary right to interpret natural law and of his ability to accomplish it. It is a once-and-for-all consent to the fact that the legislative order will determine the principles of coexistence with fellow human beings. Nonetheless, each individual retains his or her natural rights (such as personal integrity) ascribed to him or her by natural law, which remains a guiding principle in civil society. No one can renounce his natural rights because this exceeds his power, nor can he transfer more power than he possesses, since no one can justifiably exercise arbitrary power over his own existence and freedom. It is specific to man to be obliged to persevere in his

---

[53] *Ibid.*, n. 121, p. 178.

being and to be free. Consequently, from this perspective, civil liberty can only exist if it is identified with radical independence from (or resistance to) any arbitrary power that perverts the spirit of the laws and disregards the common good. And if freedom is freedom through law, and if law is fulfilled in freedom, it will be on the condition of their common manifestation as reason. There can only be justice through conformity to natural law and reason, i.e., corresponding to a freedom for the preservation of one's being and for the preservation of a free existence.

This is why, for both Suarez and Locke, the form of any government must be chosen by the political community that seeks to guarantee natural rights; and this community is the primary object of legislative power, which, under certain contractual conditions, commits to one or more representatives. The relationship between power and law in political society thus presupposes a double contract, that of the constitution of society and that of obedience to the ruler. In moving from the natural to the political condition, men continue to live in a situation of obligation, as the double contract expresses. They switch from the original obligation to obey natural law to its explicit reconfiguration as an obligation to obey civil laws, the latter being guaranteed and possibly imposed by political power through coercion. These two types of obligation share a common denominator: the unconditional obligation of men, whether in their natural condition or in their civil state, to coexist in society.

According to Suarez and Locke, this order of obligation is threefold and lies at the heart of man's path towards life in society. The first order corresponds to the obligation engendered by necessity, and it is hard to see how it could be differentiated from a constraint stemming from need and scarcity. It is, in fact, a constraint that gives rise to an obligation; indeed, the identity of needs between men produces a natural agreement, the first manifestation of which takes place in the natural society constituted by the family. Added to this is the second order of obligation, based on the agreement and suitability between human faculties and types of life in society, implying an adequacy between the ends of a fully human existence and socialization. By virtue of his freedom, his aptitude for language and reasoning, man can guarantee the continuity of social existence. The teleological organization of the world intended by Providence is continued in the human world by the universalization of obligation, without which the social bond cannot claim to last. Man's being is in the process of becoming for society, which amounts to positing a human possibility as the power of freedom; thus, man does not originally live in society, yet he must live in it to consecrate the moment of identification of natural law with the principle of reason. Finally, the third order refers to an obligation arising from an inclination, that of a tendency to live in society. This tendency is not in itself a determining power, a necessary and sufficient condition; it can only become effective when articulated to the power of freedom and reason manifested by natural law, any political society being identifiable by the consent of free men. For both Suarez and Locke, the natural and the artificial are integral to the genesis of human societies. If men cannot escape the political state, which is the only way to ensure the preservation and perpetuation of the human race, it is nevertheless up to them to institute the form of government best suited to meeting the goals set by natural law: the common good, security, and peace.

The possible justification of the historical and moral source of political power presupposes three plausible explanations: 1°) a patriarchal origin, once it has been recognized that paternal power is not identifiable with political power.[54] The father's authority, if exercised with skill and love, by force of habit and acceptance of custom, may have gradually predisposed men to one-man rule.[55] In this way, a *habitus* is established, creating the conditions for the emergence of political power through the maintenance of mutual trust, responding to the need to make life easier. 2°) The second origin relates to the theme of voluntary union. Indeed, the agreement by which men unite and integrate into a single political body constitutes political society as the product of the consent of free men.[56] If man is born free, and if no one is naturally subject to political power, then we must recognize that any partici-

---

[54] *Ibid.*, Ch. VI, n. 71, p. 151. Et n. 74, p. 152-153.
[55] *Ibid.*, Ch. VIII, n. 107, p. 170–171.
[56] *Ibid.*, n. 99, p. 166.

pation in a political society will require consent. Consent will be free because it conforms to reason, i.e., the more rationally enlightened it is, the more binding it will be. Born of moral obligation, because it expresses natural law, it can only assert itself as moral law. The political commitment is that of a freedom that poses itself as a power of coexistence, and the implication of this freedom only makes sense in the perspective of its own preservation. 3°) The last justification reminds us that power can be conquered through a just war,[57] and even, for Suarez, through an unjust war.[58] In this way, power can be legitimized by the irruption of a consensus that has historically imposed itself as the lesser evil. Nevertheless, it must always be remembered that human societies as a whole cannot be based solely on force and violence.[59] To do so would be to make the law of the strongest the only universal rule, condemning mankind to barbarism and, contradictori-

---

[57] *Ibid.*, Ch. XVI, n. 175, p. 206-207.

[58] SUÁREZ, *De Legibus*, II, 18, n. 8, p. 165.

[59] J. LOCKE, *Two treatises of government*, Book II, Ch. I, n. 1, p. 117.

ly, "and so lay a foundation for perpetual disorder and mischief, tumult, sedition and rebellion,"[60] which is what the proponents of this thesis claim to guard against.

For there to be a political philosophy, it is therefore necessary to determine another origin and justification for political power, i.e., to understand the political order in such a way that it participates in a state of law. With this in mind, Suarez summarizes the principles that legitimize political power.[61] The first title of legitimacy corresponds (when we refer to sovereign power, which has no other basis for being just than the people considered as a whole) to the immediate granting of power by God,[62] an example of which is given in the Bible with the kings Saul and David. The second is hereditary succession. Since hereditary succession does not derive from natural law, it cannot constitute the primary basis of such power. This is tantamount to recogniz-

---

[60] *Ibid.*

[61] SUÁREZ, *De Legibus* (O. O.), volume 5, Book III, 4, n. 2–3–4, p. 184–185.

[62] *Ibid.*, n. 2, p. 184–185.

ing that the first person to hold such power was granted sovereignty directly by the political community.[63] As for the third principle of legitimacy, it concerns just war and runs up against the objection that kingdoms have had no origin other than tyranny and violence, and that there can therefore be no legitimate basis for legislative power. Nevertheless, as time goes by, the people may give their consent to the new power, which is tantamount to recognizing the possibility of refounding its legitimacy through an act of popular transfer.[64] Thus, whether we consider Suarez's or Locke's position, recourse to war is a recurring historical process for the conquest of political power, which, in turn, will only gain legitimacy through the *a posteriori* consensus of the subjugated people.

---

[63] *Ibid.*, n. 3, p. 185.

[64] SUAREZ, *Defensio Fidei, O. O.*, Volume 24, Book III, 2, n. 20, p. 212.

Conclusion

At the end of this parallel between Suarez and Locke, if we consider the historical variety of political systems in terms of their origin and participation in a state of law, and starting from the theory of the double contract, social consensus appears in its relation to natural law as a necessary condition for the legitimacy of any government. From this point of view, consent to the law, in the light of freedom and the natural equality of men, has as its goal the establishment of a peaceful state, the civil state, which can only imply conformity to the law. Consequently, political society exists only because human coexistence is not reducible to force and violence, and because any power that does not actualize freedom according to law denies the specificity of politics as civility, and threatens an already possible return to despotism or barbarism; for our two authors, natural law establishes that power, apart from freedom and law, can only be inhuman, and that the absence of freedom and justice is contrary to what allows a society to call itself political, precisely because it cannot found an order of obligation. For both Suarez and Locke, the question of the genesis of political societies cannot be understood in terms of a material causality identifiable with the physical problem of a de facto power; it is inseparable from a causality through freedom, which makes it an ethical problem. The contradictory situation of the human condition: we can't live without, we can't live with, must be replaced by "we can't live without," we must therefore live with. The necessity of a founding obligation succeeds the initial impossibility.

Bibliography

AUGUSTIN, SAINT, *La Cité de Dieu*, Éditions du Seuil, Paris, 1994, traduction de L. Moreau, revue par J.-C. Eslin, 3 volumes.

BACIERO RUIZ, F. T., *Poder, ley y sociedad en Suárez y Locke. (Un capítulo en la evolución de la filosofía política del siglo XVII)*, Ediciones Universidad de Salamanca, Salamanca, 2008, CD-ROM.

BASTIT, M., *Naissance de la loi moderne*, P.U.F., Paris, 1990.

BELLARMINE, R., *On temporal and spiritual authority*, Liberty Fund, Indianapolis, 2012, edited and with an introduction by Stefania Tutino.

CARPINTERO, F., *Justicia y ley natural: Tomás de Aquino y los otros escolásticos*, Universidad Complutense, Facultad de Derecho, Servicio de Publicaciones, Madrid, 2004.

CICERON, *Des lois*, Paris, Garnier-Flammarion, 1965, traduction par Ch. Appuhn.

- *De la république*, Paris, Garnier-Flammarion, 1965, traduction par Ch. Appuhn.

COLMAN, J., *John Locke's Moral Philosophy*, Edinburgh U.P., 1983.

COUJOU, J.-P., *Droit, anthropologie et politique chez Suárez*, Perpignan, Artège, 2012.

DUCHESNEAU, F., *L'empirisme de Locke*, La Haye, Martinus Nijhoff, 1973.

DUFOUR, A., *Droits de l'homme, droit naturel et histoire*, PUF Léviathan, Paris, 1991.

DUNN, J., *The Political Thought of John Locke*, Cambridge, Cambridge University Press, 1969.

FARACO, C., *Trattato dell'Opera dei Sei Giorni. Libro Quinto*, Capua, Arteteta edizione, 2015.

FIGGIS, J. N., *Studies of political thought*, Cambridge University Press, USA, 1907.

FILMER, R., *Patriarca*, Paris, L'Harmattan, 2004, édition sous la direction de P. Thierry.

FINNIS, J., *Natural law and natural rights*, Clarendon Law series, Oxford, 1980.

GOUGH, J. W., *John Locke's Political Philosophy*, Oxford University Press, Oxford, 1950.

GOYARD-FABRE, S., *John Locke et la raison raisonnable*, Paris, Vrin, 1986.

HAAKONSSEN, K., *Natural law and moral philosophy. From Grotius to the Scottish Enlightenment*, Cambridge University Press, Cambridge, 1996.

KANT, E., *Métaphysique des mœurs. Première partie. Doctrine du droit, Introduction à la doctrine du droit*, Paris, Vrin, 1971, traduction A. Philonenko.

LOCKE, J., *Textes sur la loi naturelle, la morale et la religion*, Vrin, 1990.

- *Essais sur la loi de nature*, Bibliothèque de philosophie Politique de l'Université de Caen, Caen, 1986.
- *Two treatises of government*, Everyman's Library. Introduction by Professor W.S. Carpenter, 1982.
- *Deuxième traité du gouvernement civil*, Vrin, Paris, 1977, traduction par B. Gilson.
- *An essay concerning human understanding*, Clarendon Press-Oxford, edited with a foreword by P.-H. Niddich, 1975.
- *Essai philosophique concernant l'entendement humain*, Vrin, Paris, 1983, traduction par M. Coste.
- *Lettre sur la tolérance et autres textes*, Garnier Flammarion, Paris, 1992, traduction par J.-F. Spitz.

- *Quelques pensées sur l'éducation,* Paris, Vrin, 1992, traduction de G. Compayré.

MACPHERSON, C.-B., *The Political Theory of Possessive Individualism*, Oxford, Clarendon Press, 1962. (*La théorie politique de l'individualisme possessif de Hobbes à Locke*, Gallimard, Paris, 1971.)

MICHAUD, Y., *Locke*, Bordas, Paris, 1986.

POLIN, R., *La politique morale de John Locke*, PUF, Paris, 1960.

SKINNER, Q., *The Foundations of Modern Political Thought, 2 vol., Cambridge, Cambridge University Press, 1978 (Les fondements de la pensée politique moderne, Paris, Albin Michel, 2001, traduction par J. Grossman et J.-Y. Pouilloux).*

SPITZ, J.-F., *John Locke et les fondements de la liberté moderne*, PUF, Paris, 2001.

SUAREZ, Opera Omnia (O. O.), Éditions Vivès, Paris, 1856–1877, 28 volumes, *Opera Omnia*, Volume 3, *De opere sex dierum. De anima* (1856).

- *Opera Omnia*, Volume 5, *De legibus ac Deo legislatore (I –V)*, (1856).

- *Opera Omnia*, Volume 6, *De legibus ac Deo legislatore (VI – X). De interpretatione, mutatione et cessatione legum humanorum* (1856).

- *Opera Omnia, De gratia*, volume 7

- *Opera Omnia*, Volume 25, *In Metaphysicam Aristotelis. Disputationes metaphysicae*, (I–XXVII), (1866).

- *Opera Omnia*, Volume 26, *Disputationes metaphysicae* (XXVIII–LIV), (1866).

- *Defensio Fidei. De anglicana secta*, volume 24.

- *De Anima*, Introducción y edición crítica por Salvador Castellote, T.3 (Disp. VIII-XIV), Fundación X. Zubiri, Madrid, 1991.

THOMAS D'AQUIN, *Somme théologique*, édition coordonnée par A. Raulin, traduction par A. M. Roguet, 4 volumes, Paris, Cerf, 1984–1986.

TULLY, J., *A discourse on Property: John Locke and his Adversaries*, Cambridge, Cambridge University Press, 1978.

VIENNE, J.-M., *Expérience et raison. Les fondements de la morale selon John Locke*, Vrin, Paris, 1991.

La pensée libérale de John Locke, Caen, Cahiers de philosophie politique et juridique de l'Université de Caen, 1984, n° 5.

Other Works by the Author

31. En préparation: *L'émergence du devenir juridique de l'humanité. Vitoria.*
30. *Éthique et politique dans la philosophie du Siècle d'Or espagnol*, à paraître, 500 p.
29. *Nature humaine et pouvoir politique chez Gracian*, à paraître.
28. *From the law of nations to the emergence of international law*, USA, En Route Books, 2024.
27. *Pacte social et souveraineté politique chez Burlamaqui*, Paris, Garnier, 2024, 250 p.
26. *Ensayos sobre la filosofía del Siglo de Oro*, Madrid, Sindéresis, 2024, 300 p.
25. *Suárez dans l'histoire de la métaphysique. II, La postérité*, à paraître, Éditions Entremise, Paris, 720 p., 2024.
24. *Philosophie du Siècle d'Or espagnol. Figures de la pensée juridique et politique*, Honoré Champion, Paris, 2022, 500 p.

23. *Suárez dans l'histoire de la métaphysique. I. L'héritage. Le débat contemporain*, sous presse, Entremise Éditions Paris, 238 p., 2022.
22. *Innerarity. Éthique pour une humanité postmoderne*, préface de Daniel Innerarity, Uppreditions, Paris, 2017, 420 p.
21. *Aux origines du droit international. Le droit des gens*, Uppreditions, Paris, 2015 (2e édition 2016), 80 p.
20. *Vitoria. Le fondement éthique de la justice*, Étude et traduction, Dalloz, 2014, 427 p.
19. *Bibliografía vitoriana*, en collaboration avec M. Idoya Zorroza, Pampelune, Cuadernos de Pensamiento Español, 2014, 167 p.
18. *Droit, anthropologie et politique chez Suárez*, Artège, Perpignan, 2012, 616 p. En cours de traduction en espagnol.
17. *Pensée de l'être et théorie politique. Le moment suarézien. III*, 350 p., Louvain, Peeters, 2012, Prix Charles Lévêque de l'Institut de France, Académie des sciences morales et politiques.
16. *Pensée de l'être et théorie politique. Le moment suarézien. II*, 247 p., Louvain, Peeters, 2012, Prix Charles Lévêque.

15. *Pensée de l'être et théorie politique. Le moment suarézien. I*, 300 p., Louvain, Peeters, 2011, Prix Charles Lévêque.
14. *Bibliografía suareciana*, Cuadernos de Pensamiento Español, Pampelune, 2010, Université de Navarre, 170 p.
13. *Suárez. Quelle communauté d'être pour le Créateur et la créature ? La légitimité de la théologie à l'épreuve de la question de l'analogie de l'étant. Disputes métaphysiques XXVIII-XXIX* (Thomas d'Aquin, Cajetan, Diego Mas, Suárez), 300 p., Grenoble, Jérôme Millon, 2009.
12. *Vitoria. La question de l'homicide à la lumière du droit divin et du droit naturel. À la recherche de l'effectivité de l'exigence théologico-éthique. Leçon sur l'homicide*, traduction annotée (90 p.), 2009, Paris, Dalloz.
11. *Droit naturel et humanité chez Burlamaqui* (300 p.), avec une édition critique de l'ouvrage de Burlamaqui : *Principes du droit naturel*, 200 p., Paris, Dalloz, 2007, 500 p.
10. *Philosophie politique et ontologie. II.* (Rousseau-Kant), Paris, L'Harmattan, 2006, 207 p.

9. *Philosophie politique et ontologie. I.* (Platón, Aristóteles, Suárez, Hobbes, Spinoza), 370 p., Paris, L'Harmattan, 2006, préface de M. B. Bourgeois, de l'Académie des sciences morales et politiques.
8. Participation à l'édition intégrale digitalisée en 2004 des « Disputes métaphysiques » de Suárez en latin sur Internet (D.M. 44 et 54), sous la direction du Pr. S. Castellote Cubells, à Valence (Espagne), et en collaboration avec le Pr. J.-P. Doyle (U.S.A.), et le Pr. M. Renemann (Bochum), Internet: scc@salvadorcastellote.com, 250 p.
7. *La politique ontologique* de *Suárez. Des lois et du Dieu législateur (Livres I-II),* Introduction : « La politique ontologique de Suárez » (81 p.), Paris, Dalloz, 2003, 688 p. (2e édition, mars 2005).
6. *Suárez. Les êtres de raison et l'extension logique du champ de l'ontologie. Dispute LIV*, Introduction : « L'extension logique du champ de l'ontologie », Paris, Vrin, 2001, 204 p.
5. *Le vocabulaire de Suárez*, Paris, Ellipses, 2001, 60 p.

4. *Suárez. La généalogie d'une ontologie de l'essence. La distinction entre l'étant fini et son être. Dispute métaphysique XXXI*, Introduction : « La généalogie d'une ontologie de l'essence », Paris, Vrin, 1999, 289 p.
3. *Suárez et la refondation de la métaphysique comme ontologie* (avec la traduction de l'« Index détaillé de la Métaphysique d'Aristote »), Peeters (Philosophes médiévaux, T. 38), Louvain, 1999, 309 p. (67 p., 242 p.).
2. *Suárez et la renaissance de la métaphysique. Disputes métaphysiques I-III*, Introduction : « Suárez et la renaissance de la métaphysique », Paris, Vrin, 1998, 344 p.

Politiques de l'ontologie et horizon communautaire, Atelier national de reproduction des thèses, Lille, 1994, 2 volumes, 1er volume : pp. 1-426 ; 2e volume : pp. 427-835.

Edited Volumes:

L'État et le pouvoir, Domuni Press, Bruxelles, octobre 2016, 242 p.

Problématiques du contrat social, PU de l'ICT, 2018, 240 p.

Contributions to Edited Volumes:

- *Brill Companion to Suárez*, USA/Netherlands, Brill, 2014, 383 p. Contribution sur la philosophie politique de Suárez (Suárez's Legal and Political Thought), pp. 29–71.
- *Brill Companion on Leibniz's Thought and Activities*, 2024, *Political rationality, international balance and the duty of historical hope in Suárez (1548–1617) and Leibniz (1646–1716)* (*Rationalité politique, équilibre international et devoir d'espérance historique chez Suárez (1548–1617) et Leibniz (1646–1716)*).

About the Author

Jean-Paul Coujou, member of the Institut Michel Villey, Agrégé de philosophie chaire supérieure classe exceptionnelle, doctor (Paris I), HDR (Paris IV), honorary professor at the Faculty of Philosophy of the Institut catholique de Toulouse, where he was director of the Ethics, Philosophy, Science and Society laboratory as well as director of the doctoral cycle, is the author of some thirty books, around a hundred articles, and winner of the Prix Charles Lévêque from the *Académie des Sciences morales et politiques* in 2012. He has also been a visiting professor at several foreign universities.

www.ingramcontent.com/pod-product-compliance
Lightning Source LLC
LaVergne TN
LVHW040221110826
845146LV00005B/1362

* 9 7 9 8 8 8 8 7 0 5 5 1 3 *